T0363139

What great leaders and authors say about *Your Leadership Diamond* and working with Paul Mitchell

"*Your Leadership Diamond* is quintessentially Paul. It provides practical, actionable insights and advice for new and mature leaders, which resonate because they are 100 per cent consistent with the messages Paul has been sharing with his clients through his leadership courses and coaching for many years. Paul's brilliance is the simplicity with which he educates the reader on a topic that is often seen as complicated and even unattainable: leadership. This book is a must-read for anyone who leads teams."
Bryan Fletcher, Head of Business Processing Services, APAC Division, Credit Suisse

"This is a lovely, warm, passionate book full of practical advice to all of those who aspire to leadership. It's written in a down-to-earth, unpretentious style. It will be useful at work, at home, and in your communities. People will find advice that they can act upon and will make a difference."
Professor Gareth Jones, Visiting Professor at the IE Business School, Madrid; Fellow of the Centre for Management Development at London Business School; Partner, Creative Management Associates; author of Several Books, including *Why Should Anyone Be Led by You?*

"I've seen the impact of Paul Mitchell's work with leaders for nearly twenty years now in many organisations that I have worked in, and particularly with the evolvement of my own positive leadership style and approach since attending many of Paul's workshops. This book is a great distillation of some of the ideas and skills he has shared over those years to help leaders be the best they can be. *Your Leadership Diamond* is an essential read for those who are new to leadership, those who know it is a privilege to lead yourself and others, and those who know the power and importance of continued self-improvement."
Kate Mason, Group Director, People and Culture, Coca-Cola Amatil

"I was fortunate to come across Paul at what was a very difficult time for me and for my business. Paul's coaching and approach to becoming a better person in order to be a better leader were (and I don't use this word often) transformational. Working on the seven facets that Paul explores in his book have helped me to become a more grounded, confident, energetic, and ultimately happier CEO, husband, and father."
Stuart Grainger, Chief Executive Officer, George Weston Foods

"Paul was my coach many years ago and had a profound impact on me, helping me in so many ways through the challenges of leadership, career, and life. He since has been instrumental in helping some in my team to transform themselves and remove a great deal of anxiety and self-doubt, enabling them to step up their effectiveness as leaders. This book is the distillation of recommendations and tweaks that have enabled Paul to have such an impact on people. At a minimum, it is a very useful reminder of good practices. But most likely it may also help you transform yourself into a better version of you. An easy read and a must-read. Keep it close to reread every so often."
Alain Moffroid, Managing Director Pacific, Rentokil-Initial

"I learned so much from Paul's coaching. There hasn't been a single day over the last decade that I haven't drawn on his fantastic tools and frameworks, many of which are covered in this book. Paul's coaching was a major contributor to the sustainability and growth of our organisation. I can't thank him enough."
Suzanne Colbert, Chief Executive Officer, Australian Network on Disability

"A wise and valuable read for leaders and aspiring leaders. Paul incorporates simple models and accessible examples to which we can all relate. His approach is easy to understand and adopt and will make a measurable difference to your leadership and business results."
Anthony Brown, CEO, NobleOak Life Limited

"Paul Mitchell has supported Starlight's efforts for over a decade and has played a key role in helping transform our organisation to one that has absolute clarity of purpose, true alignment, and high engagement. Along the way, Starlight has been AON Hewitt Best employer accredited and recognised in the Top 20 Great Places to Work in Australia, both more than once; it is the only charity to be acknowledged in this space. As I read *Your Leadership Diamond*, it brings a smile to my face as I think of the devices and symbols Paul has planted in my mind—little memory tricks and symbols that are effective and that I still use. Thank you, Paul, for your contribution to my personal leadership growth and for what you have helped Starlight achieve. Your passion for and contribution to the important work of Starlight has been enormous. You have helped us to brighten the lives of thousands of children and their families' at a time when they need it most. I know this book will provide simple yet effective tools for many on their personal leadership journey. I hope you all enjoy the read!"

Louise Baxter, CEO, Starlight Children's Foundation Australia

"I have had the privilege to know Paul for the last decade. No one has the passion for the science of leadership like him. In this book, Paul shares much of his leadership wisdom. It is designed for busy people and is an easy read. It's practical and filled with golden nuggets, and it's a great reminder of the importance of constantly learning and improving in all aspects of our lives."

Daryl Sisson, Managing Director Australia and New Zealand, Thomson Reuters

"A brilliantly usable, simple, and effective toolkit for becoming a better leader written from the heart by a great mentor and coach."

Matt Gribble, Regional Managing Director Australia and New Zealand, PageGroup

"Paul's emphasis on leading in all areas of your life is exactly the sort of leadership to which we should be aspiring. He recognises that to become a better leader, you need to become a better person. The ideas in this book give you an enormous boost to take you from where you are now to where you need to be."

Marshall Goldsmith, New York Times bestselling author of *Triggers* and *What Got You Here Won't Get You There*; Thinkers 50's #1 Executive Coach

"Once again, Paul has been able to take complex leadership ideas and translate them into meaningful and practical concepts that all levels of leaders can apply to their professional and personal lives. This quick and engaging read is a great reference for all leaders interested in the link between self-improvement and improved business performance."

Hugh Lander, Chief Executive Officer, BOQ Specialist

"This book is an expression of Paul's generous spirit where he shares ways of polishing *Your Leadership Diamond*. He guides the reader, step by step, to become a pilgrim, with a pilgrim buddy, through a journey of transformation with practical skills based on thoughtful foundations. Paul's work will help those with a pre-existing awareness of their diamond to polish it better and motivate those who haven't yet found or value their own. Easy to read, food for the soul, thoughtful, practical, and applicable."

Dr Carlos A. Raimundo, Executive Coach and Inventor of the Play of Life; Author of *Relationship Capital: True Success through Coaching and Managing*

In a field littered with pretenders and wannabes, Paul stands out as a superior thinker on leadership and a superb practitioner of executive coaching. This book demonstrates his wisdom and experience, brilliantly distilled into pertinent insights and pragmatic guidance, that can be applied to bring about meaningful and relevant personal growth and change. A gem!"

Andrew Reeves, Non-Executive Director, CUA; Former Managing Director, Smith's Snackfood Company, Australia; Former CEO, George Weston Foods

All roles and organisations were accurate at the time the testimonials were provided.

YOUR LEADERSHIP DIAMOND

How to transform the way you live your life,
lead your people and leave a legacy

PAUL MITCHELL

WOODSLANE
PRESS

Woodslane Press Pty Ltd
10 Apollo Street
Warriewood, NSW 2102
Email: info@woodslane.com.au
Tel: 02 8445 2300 Website: www.woodslane.com.au

First published in Australia in 2020 by Woodslane Press
© 2020 Woodslane Press, text and diagrams © 2020 Paul Mitchell

 A catalogue record for this book is available from the National Library of Australia

Printed in Australia by McPhersons Pty Ltd
Book design by: Jenny Cowan

To Mum and Dad: thank you for your
commitment to giving back and your resilience.
To all the corporate clients and the mentors I have
worked with one on one and in groups, from my
early days as a high school teacher to my role now
as a leadership coach and author. Thank you.

And finally, to my business and life
partner of over forty years,
Deborah, who leads
straight from the
heart.

CONTENTS

PART 3: KEEP POLISHING

FOREWORD

I first met Paul when I was a young brand manager at a food company in Australia nearly thirty years ago. I was a young, South African newly arrived in Australia, and I was out to conquer the world. Paul was part of a team helping leaders, young and old, through a week-long program of self-awareness and development. I have three memories of him. One is the way his ears stuck out from his wonderfully idiosyncratic head. The second was that he taught a public speaking technique that I use to this day: he stood in front of us and asked if anyone had ever experienced something, and he raised his hand in solidarity. This motion encouraged participation, and as a speaker in my later years, it proved to be a useful nerve calmer for me. I never make a speech without asking a question of the audience and raising my hand to get agreement early on, to get the audience engaged. The third memory I have is from later in the week, when I had received some devastating feedback from a 360° feedback survey that had rocked my confidence. His humour, compassion, and perspective, gently delivered with a coolness that I appreciated because I hated being smothered, were a gift that I will always remember.

Over the years since then, my career has spanned seven countries and five continents. As the leader of multibillion-dollar companies for over twenty years, I have sought out Paul many times. Sometimes it's been on video with those cool tips on the whiteboard (such as EDI, his tool for continual improvement that I always use). As a transformational coach in the UK, in China, and most recently as the president of a large company in the United States, struggling to keep my emotional footing, I tracked Paul down again for a dose of what Paul does best: clear, direct, loving feedback with some practical tips on moving forward.

To see that he has eventually written a book that needed to be written, and that only he could write, was a joy to me, and it is my honour to write a foreword for it. Having said all of that, I was busy when I received the manuscript, and I grumbled a bit to myself as I sat on the Eurostar to Paris to meet an important client. "I had better cross the foreword to Paul's book off my list." Then as the fields of British and then French agriculture sped by my window, I read and read, and I was amazed and inspired. He has done it again: simple, engaging, funny, real, and bloody helpful.

This book is practical and simple in a way that is extremely refreshing. That Paul tackles existing myths and then suggests alternatives to them confirms the fact that he understands the very essence of humans and their strengths and weaknesses as a system.

The suggestion that you get a buddy for this journey, and the idea that small tweaks make a huge difference, is inspired. A few years ago, when I was living in China, Paul had worked with my team and had talked about the power of having a witness or buddy in your life. He has been a lifelong proponent of the idea that small tweaks over time make a big difference. I had struggled with my weight for most of my life, and so I decided to try this with my next-door neighbour. That was 2009, and since then, she and I have texted each other our weight every Wednesday. I now have two other Wednesday weight buddies, and in that time, I have made adjustments: from cappuccino to americano, from bread to rice cakes, and most recently from meat eater to non-meat eater. My weight has steadily dropped not with fanfare, but with the support of my buddies and small tweaks. These tweaks that have been imperceptible in some ways but powerful in others.

I am enchanted that he quotes Sarah Henderson, who said, "Leaders don't wait to see if there's light at the end of the tunnel. They walk down there and light the bloody thing themselves." In the section about being present, Paul talks about the South African Zulu's way of greeting each other; it was simple, super powerful, and touching, especially for me because that was my original homeland.

Pauls refusal to buy either/or is music to my ears because my latest passion is a commitment to business with purpose and a dedication to the belief that a business can be super profitable and have a deep and powerful broader purpose. In fact, the whole purpose of *the human enterprise* is to help build organisations that are truly human.

I love the seven facets of the Leadership Diamond and moving from Leading Self, through One on One, to Teams, to Clients, to the Organisation, to Family and Friends, and finally to Community. One of the many things I love about Paul is his use of memorable mnemonics. For example, his USSR model for crediting. It's easy to remember and always gives me a little giggle!

Paul's clarity about not allowing undiscussables to pollute the way you manage your team is a joy and the metaphor of 'ping pong balls above the table and bowling balls beneath' always invokes knowing, insightful smiles, and opens the opportunity to say the previously unsayable.

Even when Paul moves on to the systemic nature of organisations, he uses the same common-sense approach with mnemonics and personal experience to bring to life the bigger picture. Fancy suggesting you be a PEST to be a great agent of organisational change.

At the conclusion of this book, Paul brings us home with a connection back to family and to our place in the community. This is intensely personal and deeply grounding, and I left this book feeling grateful and hopeful.

As I approach "slowing down" age and reflect on my life as a leader in high-powered, high-status positions, it's my connection to family and my commitment to my community that concerns me most. What I love is that every piece of advice, every tweak, and every memorable rhyme or story, which serves me now, will also serve me well in the years to come.

I am so pleased that Paul has written this book and that you have chosen to read it. I look forward to hearing many stories about how this book touched your life and made a difference, just like it did for me. Can you raise your hand in agreement?

Lorna Davis, Senior Advisor to CEO Danone; Global Ambassador, B Corporation movement; Former CEO, DanoneWave; President, Nabisco; President, Kraft Foods China

PREFACE — WHERE IT ALL BEGAN

We all have a backstory.

I started working with business leaders in 1980 after many years as a district school counsellor for kids, their parents, and teachers with the NSW Department of Education, Australia. Parallel to that, I worked in two private clinics at Mosman and Neutral Bay in Sydney as a counsellor.

And years before that, I was a schoolteacher, complete with Bermuda shorts, long socks, and beige suede hush puppies. This is all long before I married and took on the roles of husband and father of two beautiful children.

But there are two threads that weave all these roles together, and I know exactly what they are, where they started, and why it's important for you to know as well.

THE FIRST THREAD

One was when I was the coach of the under-sixteen, pimple-ridden, hormone-pumped Arthur Buchan Shield Rugby Union team at Hurstville Boys High School, a Sydney suburb. It was fascinating. I was aware of kids in the classroom and their struggles to learn. Yet many of these same young men were nothing short of genius on the football field. Beautiful hand-eye coordination, superb instincts, and an uncanny capacity to read the game.

I didn't realise it then, but it was from this moment on I became intrigued, enraptured, and besotted with the human potential movement. How could it be that some of us are so gifted and talented in some areas yet struggle in others? How can some be so quick on the uptake in some environments and yet be so painfully slow in other settings? How come for so many, school is so tough, yet they excel later on in business and life itself?

To try to help answer such questions, I became an avid reader and have read thousands of books on personal development, leadership, and business. I have attended hundreds of development workshops.

One principle, one light remained flickering throughout all this seeking for truth and answers to such questions: the answers are within.

Sure, we all need a coach, a mentor, on our hero's journey to show us the way. But eventually we must find our own path into the woods and our own path out. That path is our own unique genius, our special gifts and talents that we bring to the world. All that's required to develop them to their full potential is small tweaks.

I know it's very un-Australian to brag, to toot your own horn. Yet, I think it's important for you to understand the essence of where this book has come from, and to inspire you to read and apply your learnings.

Although I'm an avid reader, I find getting through lengthy leadership books a real chore. In order to keep up momentum, I got into this habit of whenever I learnt about a great concept or idea, I'd imagine I was teaching it to an audience with a short attention span, hungry for simplicity and practicality. In other words, "Will I be able to apply this tomorrow?".

With this mindset in place, I've developed modules and hundreds of usable ideas, concepts, and skills that leaders can apply immediately to take themselves to the next level. These became the genesis of our leadership development programmes, one on one coaching, and keyshops (a combination of a keynote and workshop).

What's been even more exciting is that every time I present a usable model or technique, coaching clients and leadership development programme participants add their own small touches. The fine-tuning never ceases.

Not only that, but because many of our programmes are held over a longer time (three to six months, with our coaching assignments lasting six to twelve months), I saw first-hand their effectiveness and the impact these tools have on clients. Whether that was with teaching staff, as a corporate trainer with CIG, as an organisational development manager with St. George Building Society, as a senior consultant at Price Waterhouse Urwick, or in my own consulting practice, *the human enterprise.*

Within the overcrowded world of personal and leadership development literature, I decided to throw another rock into the pond, but this time with a difference: simplicity.

The book has been written for the leader who wants to grow and develop but doesn't have a lot of time to do so. I'm not saying there are shortcuts to success, but there are ways of shortening the time required to synthesise your learnings and start applying them to your personal and professional life. I have selected the tools, techniques and processes that leaders continue to tell us had a major impact on their leadership and lives.

THE SECOND THREAD

This is a toughie for me.

As an international trainer, coach, and facilitator, I spent a lot of time away from home. Too much. I always justified the physical and emotional distance spent in lonely five-star, luxury hotel rooms as a way of eventually creating a better life and security for the whole family. But we had a very sick daughter, Ruby. The strain on my wife, Deborah, and my son, Abe, was something I tried to hide from myself to alleviate my guilt. It didn't work.

Ruby had a rare form of epilepsy, and from around the age of seven onwards, she started having seizures that impacted her schooling, her self-esteem, and her physical health. We tried every cocktail of medications we could, we explored every diet, and we saw every mental health professional, but Ruby got sicker and sicker.

Eventually, at fifteen, we believed she was old enough to make the decision to have neurosurgery. We were told that although it was a complicated operation, there was only a very slight chance of it being unsuccessful. Ruby wanted it so badly. She hated the falling, the twisting of her head, the gaining consciousness with people staring at her and not knowing what had happened or where she was.

The operation gave Ruby and our family a sense of hope. Rubes was forever hopeful. She always told us her truth, however painful it was at times for her or for us.

At around ten, she watched the Shirley Temple movie *Now and Forever*. The little girl in the story was never to tell a lie if she proceeded what she was saying with the words "Honour Bright." It became Ruby's theme in life. You had to be true to your friends, true to your feelings, and true to yourself. She even started to tell us, out of all the various health professionals she saw, which ones were "Honour Bright" and which ones weren't.

Ruby passed away after unsuccessful surgery in the early hours of the morning on 29 September 1999. Not a day goes by when, in my own way, I both grieve for her and count my blessings that we had her in our lives for those sweet fifteen years.

There's a plaque in the school she attended in one of the gardens. It has her name on it and just two words: "Honour Bright."

Everyone copes with their grief in his or her own way. It's so personal. For months on end, I got up early with the sun barely shining, would allow myself to cry, and then got on with my day. After months of this, I knew it was not sustainable.

As many people do, I had to turn the loss of my child into something that would take me beyond my own grief and sorrow. I had a family to support both financially and emotionally, and I was drawing away from them, lost in a cocoon of my own self-pity.

I can't tell you the day or the trigger, but at some point I decided that no matter when I talked about leadership, be it one on one, in teams, or keynotes, I'd bring in the importance of spending time with family. Encouraging leaders to live a life of no regrets and to commit to being the best they could be, not just for them and their organisation, but most importantly, for their family, friends and community. That's why there are chapters on "Leading Family and Friends" and "Leading Community." Both are major threads throughout the book, reinforcing how relationships are the most important aspect of our lives.

It's only when we become better people—spouses, parents, children, siblings, and friends—that we begin to become better leaders.

THE SECOND EDITION

Welcome to the second edition of *Your Leadership Diamond*. Since I first wrote this book, we have all experienced the impact of the COVID-19 pandemic, wherever you are in the world. And it's far from over at the time we are going to print. What I do know is this; that the crisis was a chance for us all to sit back and reflect. For some, more than they have ever done before. It was an opportunity to collaborate, to co-create, to think about community way beyond our own patch and the *'slings and arrows of outrageous fortune'.*

And yet it was also a time where great fortunes could be made. I'm not talking about fortunes in regard to money. No, a whole new currency has come of age (and it's not Bitcoin). It's a currency that was always there anyway, in great families, great communities and great businesses. The currency of mutual trust and respect. For it is after times like these that we remember how people treated us, how they nurtured us, supported us - not for the money, but because they cared. Truly cared.

My wish is that as you read this edition, you will be one of those leaders. A leader who builds your reputation on the responsibility of service. That any crisis or slings and arrows you encounter will give you a chance to truly reflect on what's really important in your life. To awake the hero within and shine, not just for yourself but for others. As a result, being a leader will take on a whole new meaning for you.

> *"And in the end, the love you take,*
> *is equal to the love you make."*
> The Beatles

THE PROMISE

Welcome. If you're reading this book, it's because you're interested in living a magnificent life, being the best leader you can be, and making a meaningful contribution to your organisation and to our planet that's well beyond the bottom line. You want to take people to a better place.

First, let me under-promise and over-deliver. I can't specifically say that this book will increase your income. That said, the application of the ideas outlined have helped thousands of leaders I've worked with go on to much bigger roles, bigger paycheques, and more meaningful contributions.

But here's what I can promise: if you wholeheartedly embrace the ideas outlined and apply them diligently week by week, you will become a better person and a better leader. As we've said in the subtitle of the book, it will begin to transform the way you live your life, lead your people, and leave a legacy. Because I know who you are, and...

I KNOW WHERE YOU'RE AT

You're reading this book because you care. You really care about people and results. And you know it's not an either/or choice. Whatever you have been told or witnessed beforehand, you believe in your heart of hearts that it's possible to build a brilliant organisation with outstanding results and a passion for people. It's what I call *the human enterprise*. You're a heart-centred leader who wants results well beyond the bottom line.

As a leader, your whole being goes into maximising everyone's contribution to the strategic intent of the business and simultaneously maximising the growth, the meaning, and the joy that everyone experiences in their day-to-day work. You could be a senior leader who's been around the block a few times yet is not arrogant enough to have stopped learning or fine-tuning your leadership skills. You could be a government official who's committed to serving the public the best way you know how. You could be new to leadership and wondering where to start. You could be in your own business, with your own team. Technically you're very good at what you do, yet you need to develop your leadership skills to take yourself, your people, and your business to the next level. Whatever your role, you have this in common.

You're seeking leadership transformation.

But here's the challenge. You don't have the inclination to go to lengthy leadership development programmes, you may not have the money to invest in a personal coach, and you certainly don't have the time to learn about leadership in the next two to five years. You're looking for real results in real time, now.

If so, this book is for you. If you diligently apply the ideas and techniques in this book, you will change. The ideas have helped to change over ten thousand leaders from all parts of the globe not because they are complex, but because they are simple, tried, tested, and true.

It's your turn now.

BOOK SECTIONS

In Part 1 I look at how this book came about and share some of the philosophy I've developed over the years regarding leadership and leadership development. I outline the main model on which the book is based and overview the seven areas of focus I will be working on with you.

In Part 2 you'll find a further explanation of each facet of what we call *Your Leadership Diamond* and some specific techniques you can apply immediately for each facet. I've deliberately selected techniques for each facet that my clients repeatedly tell me have made a major difference to the way they lead at work, at home, and in their communities.

For each facet, I give you the techniques, ask you to reflect on the difference this will make to your leadership, and then end with action steps you can take. These are what I call small tweaks. A small tweak is a baby step that over time will make a big difference in your life as a leader. There are seven of them—hence seven tweaks in seven weeks. Each small tweak builds on itself. You'll continue doing all the actions, and not just for that week. You'll make them part of your ongoing personal and business rituals.

Now, I'm not expecting you to take seven weeks to read the whole book. It's a small book full of big ideas. What I do suggest is that after an initial read, you diligently go back through each chapter and, as Byron Katie says, do the work. Add one tweak every week. I've included a checklist at the end of the book to help you monitor your progress and cement the new behaviours. Rate yourself honestly and notice the change.

Initially, you'll have to get into some set routines, and this will require a little discipline upfront, but not too much. You'll get such a buzz from the application and the results gained from these tools and ideas that they'll come naturally to you. Your daily rituals and routines will become a part of who you are.

In section 3 I give some final reflections, ask you to take a stand, and encourage you to think about your leadership legacy and your own massively transformational purpose.

WHAT WILL YOU GAIN FROM YOUR SEVEN-WEEK CHALLENGE?

Everyone is different. People are at different places in their lives and in their business careers. What's ho-hum for one is transformational for another. What I can tell you is the impact these simple but elegant ideas have had on other leaders is life changing.

- Being more energised and more confident as a leader.
- Appreciating other people's talents and differences - and building lasting mutual trust and respect.
- Embracing heartfelt connections with all team members.

- Achieving awesome engagement scores.
- Experiencing the joy of providing magnificent client service and breathtaking net promoter scores (client feedback).
- Transforming the organisation into one of the industry's best.
- Truly connecting with family and friends and enriching relationships with loved ones.
- Fulfilling your soul by being involved in community work that provides some of the most meaningful experiences of all.

The biggest benefit you'll receive by reading *Your Leadership Diamond* is to become a better you. Not only will you take yourself to a better place, but you'll authentically help others get there as well. And it doesn't get much better than that.

But first, let me give you a way of getting the most out of the book to ensure your success. No one makes it on his or her own. Before you even get started, I want you to do something that will impact:

- Your buddy
- Yourself
- Our world

ENSURING SUCCESS

The chances of you reading this book and doing exactly what's outlined are fair to middling. It's an easy read, it's a short book, and the small tweaks are easy as well. But if you are truly serious about your leadership transformation, then work with a buddy to support you and keep you accountable. You'll achieve almost 100 per cent application of the ideas outlined, rapidly transform your personal and leadership effectiveness, and get even closer to your buddy personally and professionally.

The best way to have buddies support you is to support them. Get them to do the Seven-Week Challenge programme with you.

How simple is that?

Purchase or download another book immediately for them. Gift it to them. That way, you win by having an accountability buddy for seven weeks, and your buddy wins because he or she will be doing the programme—and will get you for a buddy. I win because we get an extra book sale, allowing me to spread the message of transformational leadership and creating truly human enterprises to an even larger audience.

Choose a buddy you think would enjoy doing the Seven-Week Challenge with you, who's physically present, whom you can meet with face-to-face (although virtual is okay), and whom you can check in with for ten to twenty minutes each week to track each other's progress.

You'll be amazed at the traction you get compared to other initiatives you may have started but never quite got off the ground. Remember that changing habits is a lot harder than you've imagined. An accountability buddy will help you enormously with your leadership transformation. It's what my own mentor, Dr Fred Grosse, calls scaffolding, a support structure to build new habits until they're firmly in place.

In the majority of *the human enterprise's* Leadership Development Programmes, I always introduce participants to their imaginary buddies. It's a bit like your imaginary rabbit, horse, or playmate you had as a little kid. We even give your new buddy a name and get you to put your arm around their imaginary shoulders.

The name of that buddy is EDI. Now, that could be Edweena or Edward; we'll leave that up to you. But this buddy will do more for your success and continuous striving for excellence than any other friend you've ever had. Here's how you use EDI.

You and your buddy will write down and share your specific commitments for that week, as well as the previous tweaks you've been working on. That's when you bring in EDI and take it in turns to discuss:

E   What's been EXCELLENT?
Where have you done well this week?
What have you achieved?

D   What do you need to DEVELOP?
Where do you need to improve?
What didn't happen?

I   What are some IDEAS to work on?
What's excellent that you can build on,
and what needs to be addressed in the
next week?

In fact, EDI itself is a great leadership tool for any one-on-one or group meetings where you want to discuss progress of any sort. It's a process review tool.

- Notice it starts with the positives, or appreciative inquiry (Excellent).
- It then moves onto continuous improvement (Develop).
- Followed by the generation of ideas (Innovation).

HERE YOU GO

Sit down, relax, take some quality time, and take it in turns to find out what's important to you and your buddy, what you both stand for, and how you can move each other ahead in your respective worlds. Take each other to a better place.

But before you do, it's vital to have not only the right buddy but also the right mindset and empowering beliefs to get you there. In order to help you here, let's bust some of the myths around leadership development to power you up.

PART 1
DIGGING FOR DIAMONDS

COLLECTIVE MYTHS REGARDING LEADERSHIP DEVELOPMENT

There's a rumour going around that real leadership is the domain of the chosen few, and that it takes almost superhuman powers and personality traits to lead. In fact, you'll even hear people say, "Oh, no. I could never be a leader." That's ridiculous.

There are many reasons for this paradigm, but I will share three myths that are often swallowed but aren't true. Frankly, they make it harder for you than it needs to be to enhance your leadership effectiveness. It's as if we've gone into a cultural trance and have been hypnotised into believing them.

THE THREE MYTHS

1. Leaders are born, not made.
2. Leadership is complicated.
3. It takes a lifetime to learn to lead.

It doesn't have to be this way. Come out of your trance *now* for your awakening.

Let's bust all three myths. I want you to truly believe you can transform your leadership in seven weeks. But like anything in life, your mind set—your belief that it's possible—is essential to your results. So here are three alternative beliefs that I'd like you to call your very own, at least for the next seven weeks.

1. Anyone can lead; it's a choice.
2. Leadership is simple (although not easy), but it's as complicated as I want to make it.
3. I can dramatically transform my leadership in seven weeks and continue to refine it for the rest of my days.

Let's now look at these alternative beliefs one by one.

Empowering belief 1: *anyone can lead; it's a choice*

You really can lead from any chair. It's a choice. You don't need the title of leader on your business card. In fact, positional power used too often can erode your leadership and true connection to others. Power really does reduce empathy. Sure, you'll get people doing what you ask, but it will be out of compliance ("have to" energy) rather than commitment ("want to" energy). The real power rests with the people doing the work.

And what about the question of leaders being born, not made? Well, I've never seen a leader who wasn't born, and neither have you. They are all born. But I've never bought into the concept of a born leader. Leadership is a mindset and set of skills, both of which can be learned. It's about leaving people, places, and processes better than you found them. It's the receptionist who looks at the poor service of the current courier company, checks out their prices, and then researches and recommends a better option to management. That's a leadership chair. Again, you can lead from any chair.

But I do have a caveat to this. Some families and environments give our kids a better chance at picking up leadership skills somewhere down the track. In the home where the parents keep telling their kids how much they are loved, how unique they are (balancing this with how we are all flawed in some way), and how important it is to give back and to contribute, these kids definitely have a head start at being "servant" leaders, as Robert Greenleaf calls them in *Servant Leadership*.

But many Senior Leaders tell me "Paul, we can't all be leaders, some of us have to be followers." Well, why not be both? In fact, I believe you can never really be a good leader unless you've also learnt to be a good follower. The more senior you are, the more you have to continually check that you're leaving your ego at the door. A big dose of humility trumps a big dose of hubris every time.

So make a choice. Make it your choice to lead.

Empowering belief 2: *leadership is simple - it's as complicated as I want to make it*

> *"Any intelligent fool can make things bigger*
> *and more complex ... it takes a touch of genius and*
> *a lot of courage to move in the opposite direction."*
> Albert Einstein

You may have read thousands of articles on leadership, read hundreds of books, and been to the odd workshop or two. But I can guarantee when talking about leadership, they all say pretty much the same things:

- You've got to know where you are now (face reality).
- You've got to get clear on where you're going, including a better place and a bigger place (have a vision).
- You've got to plan how you're going to get there and overcome the roadblocks you'll encounter along the way (know the path).
- You've got to determine the time, energy, money, and people required to do so (know the resources).
- You've got to excite others and yourself to exceptional performance along the way (engage the people).
- You've got to constantly adjust your sails (have behavioural flexibility).

That's it. It's that simple. Now, notice I didn't say it was easy. Not at all. But it's not as complicated as it's made out to be. Sure, each of those steps involves a lot of work and sub-steps, and the execution can't always be perfected, but again, it's not that complicated.

It becomes complicated because we lose heart, we lose focus, we lose us, and we forget who we are and who we can be. In this book, you'll learn about the concept of *Leaders for Life* which will help you with that focus. It will help with keeping your energy and the energy of others around you alive.

Leadership is an attitude and a set of skills, both of which you can learn. All it takes is practice, practice, practice.

Empowering belief 3: *I can dramatically transform my leadership in seven weeks and continue to refine it for the rest of my days*

This book won't make you the US president or the head of Apple in seven weeks. That may take a little longer. And it's not even the individual tweaks by themselves that do it. It's the compounding effect of those small tweaks over time.

> "*Compound interest is the eighth wonder of the world.*"
> Albert Einstein

Mathematically, it works like this: if you get 1 per cent better and keep doing that 1 per cent daily, it won't take you one hundred days to get 100 per cent better. It will only take seventy. That's the power of compounding.

Frankly, I think seventy days is too long. What I can promise is a significant improvement, a transformation in the way you lead, in seven weeks That's forty-nine days, or a little over a month and a half. This is provided that you faithfully learn and apply each skill or idea and then continue to build on them week by week.

Because the model we'll be sharing takes in all facets of leadership, including leading you, leading in business, and leading in your bigger life, you'll be blown away at the energy and focus you develop, as well as the difference in how you feel about yourself, being a leader, and the results you obtain.

At the majority of our Leadership Development Programmes, I ask participants to commit to small tweaks they can do after each session. I then walk the room winding a small music box. People can barely hear it. Participants strain their ears to try to pick the tune.

At the end of the programme, I reintroduce the music box and, while turning it, let participants know that the real measurement of their success will be how much they continue to turn their small tweaks into commitments following the programme. I say that at first, like the music box, their small tweaks may be indistinguishable, and they'll hardly notice them.

I then place the music box on a table, saying that the table represents time and that every small tweak over time will amplify. It will crescendo. I play the music box again, but this time, the volume that's produced is dramatically louder. The formula is very simple: small tweaks (the music box) over time (the table) create big results.

Your path to success won't be without challenges, even with the right mindset. Therefore, before we get going, let's look at some typical roadblocks you may encounter as you become the best leader you can be. Once you're aware of them, it's so much easier to address them, overcome them, and blast them out of the water.

If you can mention it, you can manage it.

ROADBLOCKS AND BARRIERS TO YOUR SUCCESS

Again, I've promised you that leadership transformation is simple, not easy. It gets even easier if upfront you're aware of the potential roadblocks. There will definitely be roadblocks; after working in the leadership development space for more than thirty-five years, you see patterns. Success leaves clues, and so do failure and disappointment, with the same roadblocks and barriers surfacing again and again. Now, not every roadblock I'm about to reveal may be true for you. Nothing holds true for every leader, and roadblocks won't appear every time with everyone and everywhere. They do, however, appear with enough predictability and regularity that it's a reasonably safe bet to call them patterns. And they all start with one big pattern or problem: this fascination we all seem to have with *choice*.

It's either this or that, one or the other, A or B, change or stability, risk or safety. You can't have your cake and eat it too. Well, bollocks to that. It seems that having to choose is in our DNA. If you're a *Matrix* fan, it's "Take the blue pill or the red pill." In *Alice in Wonderland*, it's Alice's question to the Cheshire Cat: "Which road do I take?" Humour is even based on this. If you're a Monty Python fan, you know the big question: "Crucifixion or freedom?" In my own business, business coaches have told me that I sell either services or sell products. But why one or the other? Why not both?

Well, here's the solution: *refuse to choose.*

The choice dilemma was beautifully picked up in Dr Jim Collins's research in *Built to Last,* where he articulated that poor leaders deliberate and pontificate over what seem to be diametrically opposed options. This or that. It often leads to real stress and poor performance. He called this "the tyranny of the *or.*" That is the logical view that cannot easily accept the paradox of not being able to live with two seemingly contradictory ideas at the same time.

So many times, I hear in service firms, "Look. I either do my billings or serve my clients." *Gong.* As the beautiful Robin Williams would say, "Thank you for playing!"

Refuse to choose. Rather than thinking one or the other, you creatively combine both options. I believe it was Jim Collins who coined the alternative phrase "The genius of the *and*, rather than the tyranny of the *or.*"

This *and* that. It's the leader *and* follower genius we spoke of earlier.

So what are the choices leaders grapple with as leaders— choices that require an *and* mindset, not an *or* mindset?

THE THREE CHOICES

There are three big choices that I see leaders struggle with, at times at a conscious level and sometimes unconscious, and that stunt their development and success. Do you recognise yourself in any of them?

- Choice 1: skills or passion?
- Choice 2: results or people?
- Choice 3: work or life? (Yep, the old work-life balance furphy.)

Let's look at these in more detail and show why choosing doesn't help you and actually detracts from your leadership brilliance.

Choice 1: skills or passion

There's a real problem in a lot of leadership development activities. I've fallen for it myself as a coach, trainer, and facilitator over the years. We teach people skills. What? Yep, we teach people skills. You say, "But surely it isn't this what they want? Isn't this what they need?" Well, sort of, but it's only half the story.

It's wrong to send a changed person back to an unchanged environment. I can't believe how many leaders I've sent back into their corporate worlds with the four steps for this, the five steps for that, and the seven steps for the other. Hey, nothing wrong with skills, of course, but imagine this. Your manager has just returned from Leadership School and learnt the Seven-Step Delegation Process. Now she's going to go through it with you no matter what. So, don't interrupt.

Can you see the problem? We think the skill steps are the answer, and the more military precision we can do them with, the better. Often, it's because the other person needs to improve her performance, her responsibility, or her urgency. In fact, in some way you're going to teach them a lesson. But let me assure you if it's just the skill steps you deliver, it will be you who will be less on. You need to also connect to your heartfelt intention, or as my good mate Steve Koumoulas from VividMath says, you need to be more "on" as a leader. The skills will get us the results, but of course they're only half the story.

You're not a robot, and neither is the person in front of you. Leadership is about a relationship: the one you're in right now!

Use the skills as a platform, as a guide. Remember that you're talking with a real person. You can't just go through the motions. You need to relate and connect with them. Be more "on".

Let yourself come through.

At *the human enterprise*, we deliver a BlessingWhite programme called "Why Should Anyone Be Led by You? What It Takes to Become an Authentic Leader." In it, Professors Goffee and Jones articulate this idea of "being on" as "be yourself ... more ... with skill." Get it? The "more of yourself" is your passion, your emotions, your values, and the "with skill." Well, that is your behaviour.

But don't get too cocky. In our Transformational Leadership Coaching, we not only focus on the behavioural change of the leader—their outer game—but also their mindset, their beliefs, their shadow, or the things that could be sabotaging their success. This is what Timothy Gallwey refers to as the inner game in his book *The Inner Game of Golf.*

The very opposite side of this is true as well. If the leader thinks it's going to be all about the relationships, the feelings, the connection between us, or "the vibe of the thing," then you also have a potential problem. Vital as this is, as honourable an intention it upholds, it can also cause a lot of damage.

Can you imagine someone with a wonderful, loving, giving, generous intention and an unbelievable passion about to do open heart surgery on you? But what if he or she has no skills? Uh oh—dangerous!

This is the choice many leaders think they have to make. They say,

"That's just who I am."

"I just want to be myself."

"I just want to be me."

"I don't want to come across as phoney."

"I could never follow a strict formula, it's just not me."

Well, I'll let you in on a secret. The skills don't *FREEZE* you—the skills *FREES* you. In other words, they don't stop you in your tracks. They actually allow you to be more of yourself.

There's no better evidence of this than in the sporting arena. For example, a tennis player may perfect a certain stroke after hours and years of practice, so much so that she doesn't even have to think about it anymore; it's unconscious. This is the old ten thousand hours rule. It allows the conscious mind to focus on all the other elements that are present in order to not just execute the shot but plan it perfectly in relation to all the other elements that are happening (the wind, the opponents' weaknesses, the next shot).

We need to know the skills backwards and then add our passion. But there's a problem if we just choose one or the other. It's a bit like this:

Skills without passion = lack of impact

Passion without skills = lack of focus

If you focus solely on developing your skills and not on developing your passion by being true to you, showing enough of yourself, and really connecting, then you'll never quite make the impact you are capable of.

No impact.

No results.

No progress for you or the organisation.

No better place to which you're taking people.

On the other hand, if it's all about you—your passion, your commitment, your unbridled enthusiasm—without the skills, personal control, and a more systematic, considered approach, then let's face it: you're everywhere.

No focus.

No clarity.

No progress for you or the organisation.

No better place to which you're taking people.

How do you do both? We'll get to that later, but for now, refuse to choose.

Choice 2: results or people

I'm an easy-going bloke, I'm chilled, and I'm laid-back most of the time—but this one is giving me a dose of it.

It's unbelievable that we still have to make the case for employee engagement even with very senior leaders. Despite literally hundreds of research papers, some managers still don't get the engagement equation. Admittedly, they may have been burnt because engagement is a necessary but not sufficient condition for great performance.

In other words, we can all be engaged, but that doesn't mean we are necessarily going to produce excellent results over time. But here's the rub: try getting consistent, excellent results over time without engagement. Look at it this way: full engagement doesn't necessarily lead to a great result, but a lack of engagement certainly leads to a poor one.

One of my favourite equations is the following.

By all means, do your engagements surveys. But let me assure you that engagement is an emotion, not a number. If you want more emotion and more feeling in your business, it starts with you. It takes what US Navy SEALs Jocko Willink and Leif Basin call extreme ownership. If you want your followers to emotionally connect with what they are doing, to take ownership, then first connect with your own emotions, your personal energy, and your ability to energise.

In fact, it's why I believe so many engagement surveys have got it wrong, reinforcing dependency, rather than personal responsibility. For example, most engagement surveys include such questions as:

1. "My manager gives me performance related feedback."
2. "I have the resources to do my job well."
3. "I'm told the Mission and Vision of my company."

What do you notice here? All these questions are "other" dependent. That is, they rely on the proactivity of the manager rather than the personal responsibility of the respondent. Now, I don't want to diminish the importance of leaders responding to survey feedback. But I do want to provocatively challenge the way that many of them are structured.

Many surveys are worded in a way that suggests you are waiting for others to take action in order for you to be engaged. Surely, it's a two-way street. Where is the ownership here? What if we flipped the questions to:

1. "I actively seek performance related feedback from my manager"
2. "I continually ask for the resources I need to do my job well"
3. "I constantly seek clarity on the Vision, Mission and Values of my organisation"

Different story eh! These are all proactive 'self' questions.

I'm not saying managers don't have a part to play here. Of course they do. The analogy I use is that of a runabout boat with two outboard motors. One is the individual and one is the company, or the individual's manager. If one of the motors is running, and left to itself, the boat will have a tendency to just go around in circles. It's only when both are working together that it's "full speed ahead".

And please, please, please, don't even think about doing another engagement survey if you are not going to act on the feedback from the last one. Don't scratch your head wondering why the results are even worse, or the response rate is dismally low. It's imperative to be very visible about how your plans are linked to the feedback you got last time. Your people must see that their voice counts.

On the other end of the spectrum, many organisations have taken up the engagement torch and got lost in the inferno. They have summed up their aspirations and ambitions for their people as "The ABC Company—a great place to work." There's no way I want to detract from that. What a great ambition and a brilliant way to help create *the human enterprise*. But I'll never forget a presentation by the onetime CEO of an international IT organisation in Australia. He was a big guy with a deep voice. He was no fuss, to the point, and had a thick Scottish accent. He also had two big dogs. He spoke to the leadership cohort I was working with and beautifully summed up his thoughts on engagement. "A great place to work," he said in a drawn-out breath. "I'll tell you what a great place to work is. A great place to work is a profitable one. Try working at one that ain't."

If you've been around the block a bit, you'll know exactly what he means. Profit is the fuel for growth, both for the growth of the business and the people that work there.

Yet at an unconscious level, leaders still feel they must choose between focusing on results or focusing on people.

It's a mistake I made as a young teacher early in my career. I was determined to get close to the year eleven and year twelve students. "Call me Mitch," I remember saying, thinking this would show that I was one of them. But they didn't want me to be one of them. They wanted me to be the teacher, with all the stuff that came with it. They wanted me to lead. I can imagine what they were thinking: *Here we go again, another try-hard. Come in, spinner.*

I so wanted to be their friend, wanted to be accepted, that I forgot what I was there for. This doesn't mean we don't work with people in a respectful manner. It means that if your need to be accepted is greater than your need for results, then you've got a real problem.

As a leader, being liked is a bonus. Being respected is essential.

This is why so many new leaders struggle when first placed in a leadership role, like me as a newbie schoolteacher. For Pete's sake, I was only four years older than most of my students, and quite frankly, I identified more with them than with most of the Bermuda-panted, long-socked, hush puppy–wearing, middle-aged teachers in the staff room. (By the way, I soon began to dress like this as well. Never underestimate the power and influence of the environment you are in! But that's for another day.) Unless he is very self-aware, a new supervisor, particularly if he is promoted internally, may want to stay a member of the gang that he was recently a part of, the gang from which he was promoted. He desperately tries to avoid conflict, to keep the peace, and to avoid performance issues or potential discomfort. It's all about relationships. The fear of rejection is stronger than the flame of results.

My take on it is this: keep putting relationships ahead of results, and pretty soon you'll have none of both.

Sure, we're all happy campers, working "dry cleaning hours" (in by nine and out by five), but what if the results are not there? Eventually, costs will have to be cut, and often the first thing to go is people. So in some ways, when leaders don't make the tough calls from a long-term perspective, you could easily argue that they don't really care about the people. All they really care about is not feeling guilty, feeling judged, and not being liked. I call it being too NICE.

Nothing
Inside
Cares
Enough

If you really cared, you'd give the feedback to help the other person grow. Don't be so arrogant that you think people can't take your feedback or that they have stopped learning. How dare you deny someone of their growth. No, we need to go from NICE cultures to REAL cultures.

Recognise
Everyone's
Ability to
Learn

Then there's the other side of it: the manager who wants results, and that's it. No time for the niceties, the process, the relationships. "Show me the money!" as the film *Jerry McGuire* says. John Cleese was even cruder in his film about performance appraisal feedback when describing result-orientated leaders.

Apologies to all those expecting, but he said, "Don't tell me about the labour pains—show me the baby."

Many of the leaders I coach often come with this extreme results focus. They've been amazingly successful with brilliant technical results and have been promoted, because of these results. But now it's time for a bigger role and their sponsors can see a major problem mounting on the horizon: THEY WRITE PEOPLE OFF TOO QUICKLY. Their mantra is *"I don't tolerate fools gladly"* For them, the good performers, the smart ones, they're great, no trouble at all. But they quickly write off the performers, that in their eyes, are too slow.

The trouble with that view is that no-one is a great performer all the time, and people often need time, feedback and coaching (relationship focus) to improve.

Keep writing off people off and there'll eventually be no one left.

The key to great leadership, then, is make relationships *and* results count. That's what we call the human enterprise.

Great relationships, but never at the expense of results. And great results, but never at the expense of great relationships. It's more than a bet each way—it is *the* bet.

It's not Mitch or Deborah, my wife; that's not the marriage. Those are two elements of the marriage. It's Mitch *and* Deb together making the marriage. It's the marriage of relationships and results that the leader is after.

Although many books have been written with the theme of people who feel good about themselves produce good results, I can tell you it's essential to also remember that the opposite is also true and is one of Mitchell's laws: people who produce good results feel good about themselves.

Again, it's about people and results. Fess up. If you're too much of a softy (too NICE), then toughen up. Push for those results. Get REAL. If you're too results orientated, suffering from the cannibal syndrome ("fed up with people"), then chill, relax, and stop judging everyone around you as "less than."

Just remember the old standard, evergreen definition of leadership: getting results through people.

Choice 3: work or life

"A master in the art of living draws no distinction between his work and his play, his mind and his body, his education and his recreation. He hardly knows which is which. He simply pursues his vision of excellence through whatever he is doing and leaves others to determine whether he is working or playing. To himself, he always seems to be doing both."
James Michener

I think that quote says it all. No doubt you've heard the expression "work-life balance" many times before, and it's particularly relevant if you've visited some so-called Third World countries. When most people do, they are often blown away by the juxtaposition of levels of having and levels of happiness. Through our First World lens, you'll often hear the expression, "These people have absolutely nothing, but they're so happy." Dig a little deeper, and you'll find another pattern. It's a pattern I see with the most successful and happy leaders

I work with: they don't delineate between work and life. They simply live. It's all life to them.

But why do we insist on balance? Think about this. If you were doing something you loved, mixing with great people and making a difference, and feeling really fulfilled, where's the imbalance?

My point is the work-life balance protagonists have swallowed another furphy without ever realising it. It's the assumption (on the extreme) that work is crap and that you need a break from it to balance out the horror. "All work and no play makes Jack (or Jill) a dull boy (or girl)."

Well, what if you love your work? What then? Now, I'm not saying spend all your time at work. Far from it—I realise we all have family and friends, and I'm a huge believer in spending as much time with them as possible. But I am saying that work can be fun. In fact, if it's not fun, is it worth it? Another of Mitchell's laws is "The purpose of business is to give us more life, not to suck the life out of us."

A lot of my time spent coaching leaders, particularly senior leaders, is trying to shake this paradigm. They think because they are senior leaders, they have to put in the hours, have to make the sacrifices, have to suck it up, have to be so bloody serious. But often they're miserable as hell. Even worse, their whole identity is around their job. And what's left when that goes? A big, ugly black hole that some may call depression.

How different would it be if they willingly chose to occasionally put in the hours, didn't see the extra effort as a sacrifice, and were in awe of their work and the people around them? See yourself as a servant to some bigger cause, some bigger meaning. Make it your quest to take people to a better place. Learn to love your work and see it as part of your life, not separate from it. Or, if you can't love your work, don't accept that "it's just the way it is." Do something about it.

Please, please don't spend your life's energy doing something you don't like with people you don't like, feeling that you don't make a difference. Life is far too short. If you see your work as part of your life, you'll also see your role as a leader as part of your life. You'll get the importance of leading in all aspects of your life. The mindset of simultaneously achieving success and significance will open endless possibilities of purposeful potential. You will truly become a *Leader for Life*.

Make your magnificent work part of your magnificent life. Make it about the integration of work and life, not the balance of it.

Go for work-life harmony.

I've mentioned it a few times, and you may be scratching your head and thinking, "What's a *Leader for Life*?" Let me explain exactly what I mean.

LEADERS FOR LIFE

Throughout this book, I refer to the concept of *Leaders for Life*. This mentality is at the heart of everything we do at *the human enterprise*. It's the mindset that once you make the decision to lead, it's a lifetime commitment to reaching your own potential and helping others reach theirs.

EVERYONE

Leaders for Life is about how everyone can lead, irrespective of whether they have it in their job title. You'll hear me repeat many times in this book that you can lead from any chair. In fact, you can lead every time.

EVERY TIME

It's so easy to play the victim or to convince yourself and others that your hands are tied, there's nothing you can do, and it's out of your control. Sometimes—though I think rarely—that is the case. It does mean sometimes accepting that things are the way they are, that we can't change them. But not for leaders.

They genuinely believe they can always make a difference, they can always do something, they can always have a go.

> *"We are the ones we've been waiting for."*
> Barack Obama

Leaders don't wait around until someone else does something or makes things better. I always remember attending a presentation by Australian icon Sarah Henderson, who ran one of Australia's largest cattle farms in the Northern Territory. She closed her presentation by saying, "Leaders don't wait to see if there's light at the end of the tunnel. They walk down there and light the bloody thing themselves."

EVERYWHERE

Leaders for Life lead in their organisations, with their family and friends, and in their communities. Great leaders know that leadership is not just limited to something within their organisation. Leadership is so much more than just vision, strategy, KPIs, and performance reviews. A leadership mindset isn't a car you park at the front door when you walk into your home. It's not a coat or dress that you take off and hang in your wardrobe on Friday evening. Just as you can lead from any chair, from the chairman to the receptionist, your leadership chair can also be a kitchen chair, a dining room chair, or even a park bench. A genuine leadership mindset is just as important at home and in your community as it is in business.

Leaders for Life realise the hypocrisy of putting all their efforts into developing others at work, having them reach their full potential, and yet neglecting the cries and help from family and friends. Their children wait for them to come home and watch *Frozen* for the twenty-eighth time. Success at work will never compensate for failure in the home. *Leaders for Life* take their commitment to leading in their families and communities very passionately, just as they do their commitment to their organisations.

EVERY BIT

Every bit of their being—notice I didn't say *doing*—is linked to making people, places, and projects better than they found them. *Leaders for Life* are energised by knowing that they can make a difference, that their efforts count. They give every bit of themselves towards that goal.

They're energised. You can feel that energy field around them because every part of their being shouts,

"We can do this together."
"Things will get better."
"The possibilities are endless."

They really get what Napoleon Bonaparte meant when he said, "A leader is a dealer in hope." Along with countless others, they make their daily "To Do" list, and they also decide on who they are going to be that day, what part of them needs to show up. They have their daily "To Be" list: appreciative, authentic, courageous, inspiring, reflective, assertive. And every bit of their behaviour stems from these decisions on the way they want to show up. They realise that beliefs are simply choices or decisions they make. They're clear on their values; who they are, warts and all; and who they need to become. They know skills and techniques are important but only up to a point. They don't marry the doing and divorce the being. They realise the importance of both.

When you behave like this as a leader, you're bound to have more energy. You're not putting effort into being someone you're not, or continually trying to prove how great you are or how you're the smartest one in the room.

EVERY GENERATION

Being a *Leader for Life* is not about how great you are—it's how great you leave the place or the people around you. And that means your main role as a leader is to develop a leadership mindset within everyone you touch. At *the human* enterprise, part of our mission statement is to develop cultures where everyone leads. These days they call it distributed leadership. It's not just the prerogative or exclusive right of top management. In a corporate sense, it's making sure you're continually developing "bench strength" and not just in your high-potential or talent programmes. With family and friends, it's helping them strive to reach their full potential. In your community, it's helping to keep the torch burning for your favourite charity long after you've departed. Great leaders produce more leaders, not more followers.

EVERY MINDSET

Can you imagine if everyone had the mindset of whatever came up at work or home simply stated, "OK, this is what it is. How can I make it better?" What a difference that would make. Well, that's precisely what *Leaders for Life* do: they realise that no one makes it on their own, that it's only through ongoing work with others that anything of greatness is achieved.

In fact, although they're self-assured and confident, *Leaders for Life* don't give off the arrogant pheromone. There's a humility about them that tacitly makes us followers realise we have to play our part as well. We realise that we can grow, we can make mistakes, and we will carry on long after they have gone through their nurturing of us. In fact, *Leaders for Life* know it's not about empowering followers; the power is already within them. It's about inspiring followers to take the power that's there and lead.

When *Leaders for Life* leave the room, it doesn't fade into darkness. The light shines brighter. You want to light up a room when you enter it, not when you leave it.

HOW BEING A LEADER FOR LIFE WILL ENRICH YOUR LIFE

This will be different for all of us, but here's what I can tell you. If your primary identity is not attached to your job, you're going to be OK. You're going to bounce back, no matter what your results or what the world throws at you. If your primary identity is connected to your job, you're going to suffer—maybe not now, but you will eventually. Every time the figures go up and down, so will you. Every time there's a failure, you'll feel like a failure. Every time you come across difficult times in your business, you'll feel that life is difficult, and that's going to prevent you from being a great leader.

The same is true in your personal life. If your self-worth is tied to your net worth, as soon as you lose money or you make a poor financial decision, it's not just your net worth that suffers. Your self-worth also suffers. Tie your self-worth to something more than just work. That way, you're going to be able to weather most storms.

Being a *Leader for Life* means you have a frame of reference through which to see issues. I remember when one of my clients had some production problems at his plant, and everyone was panicking about being out of stock. He reminded everybody, "It's only ice cream. We're not solving world peace or eradicating world hunger here." Being a *Leader for Life* will help you put the leadership issues you face at work into perspective.

To be successful these days requires you to proactively manage the many distractions you'll face within your own organisation and the marketplace. This requires you to innovate. Innovation's twin is the possibility of failure. If you take failure personally—that is, "I failed, and so I am a failure"—it will be very difficult to innovate.

We all have a fear of failure at some level. Knowing life is much bigger than just business will help you push this fear of failure to one side. It will enable you to take risks that you otherwise may not have taken if your identity is too strongly connected to your business performance.

Have you noticed that when things aren't going well at work, if home is settled and if home is your sanctuary, it seems to put everything into perspective? You can still wake up in the morning feeling grounded, with the energy required to continue adding value. This only happens if you're a *Leader for Life*.

On the flip side, you're also going to have some spectacular results in your life. Again, if your identity is tied to them, you can easily get carried away. It's seductive. You can get high on it and not realise your own hubris. I've been there. When I finally broke through in my business, I went out and purchased a sports car, a two-door Datsun 240Z. I fell in love with it at first sight. I didn't even do a mechanical inspection on it. Hey, I knew enough about cars. Within a month, I took it to my brother, who really knows his stuff. He inspected it, cut out the rust on the floor, and welded the car back together. He handed me back a piece of the rusted floor in a plastic bag with a note:

> *"For over a thousand years, Roman conquerors returning from the wars enjoyed the honour of a triumph— a tumultuous parade.... A slave stood behind the conqueror, holding a golden crown, and whispering in his ear a warning—that all glory is fleeting."*
> From the 1970 film *Patton*

Being a *Leader for Life* will keep you grounded. It will help you make more realistic decisions, rather than thinking you can do no wrong. It will inspire you to really connect with everyone in your organisation at all levels.

> *"Or walk with kings—nor lose the common touch."*
> Rudyard Kipling

It will get you clear on your values, clear on what you stand for, and clearer on who you are well beyond your title, function, or organisation. Knowing what your values are and being true to them during those dark nights of the soul is what will pull you through.

> *"This above all: to thine own self be true."*
> William Shakespeare

Because when you're true to you, when you are aligned with your values, you'll have an inner strength and compass that guides your every decision. Making a stand will be easy. My grandfather used to say, "If you don't stand for something, you'll fall for anything." With the onset of the coronavirus pandemic, we were presented with many choices as leaders and stands we could make.

- Were we going to be extreme optimists and pretend that all this will pass very quickly?
- Were we going to be pessimists, predicting the end of mankind as we know it?
- Were we going to be victims and feel helpless? Were we going to pause or make knee jerk reactions?
- Were we going to contract as quickly as we can?

FROM		TO
Pessimist	＞	Pragmatist
Helpless	＞	Helpful
Panic	＞	Prosperity
Contraction	＞	Expansion

As hard as this may seem, it all gets down to one thing, being useful, making a difference, being there for others.

Finally, we live in a world of speed. Everyone wants it faster, better, and cheaper. I can absolutely assure you that the faster, best, and cheapest way of becoming a better leader is to become a better person.

I'd love you to join me in my stand of leading in all areas of your life and experiencing the joy and energy you create for yourself and those around you.

Now that we've blown some of the myths about leadership, looked at some potential roadblocks, and given you a feel for what it takes to be a *Leader for Life* and how it will enrich your life, let's look at *Your Leadership Diamond*. The model will help you identify exactly where you need to start shining and give you a few ideas on how to do this along the way. It's the very heart of this book.

YOUR LEADERSHIP DIAMOND — AN OVERVIEW

As you're probably aware, diamonds didn't start off as diamonds. They were big lumps of coal in the ground, and with enough pressure on them, the coal transformed into diamonds. It's referred to as a 'dissipative structures' in *Leadership and the New Science* by Margaret Wheatley.

I know you've had a lot of pressure on you over the years; we all have. In fact, we've had it since birth. Some of it is good, and some of it is not so good. Your parenting, your siblings, your schooling, your country of birth, your ethnic background, your religion, your upbringing, your studies, your jobs, your relationships, your role as a leader from school to now, and the variety of good and not-so-good experiences along the way. Let's face it: you're no longer just a lump of coal.

So, how do you see yourself? Well, to me, you're a diamond. And no, I didn't say a rough diamond. You already have everything you need inside of you to shine. All the answers are truly within. You simply have to find them.

You are the leadership diamond.

This way of thinking about leadership is a radical shift from what we have been taught for years. That we are missing something, and that the something has to come from outside of us. That the name of the game is self-improvement. It feeds on what many leaders, from frontline supervisors to CEOs, carry with them daily: their own variety of NOGOES, disguised in all shapes and forms and keeping them from being all they can be.

NOt
GOod
Enough**S**

Their NOGOES means they have to constantly prove themselves to their own bosses, their peers, their teams, and most of all to their own parents, who in many cases may have left this earth years ago. Not that there's anything wrong with achievement, with striving, with going for excellence. But there's a big difference when doing it for yourself, for you to be all you can be, and to be the best leader you can, versus trying to prove yourself worthy in the eyes of somebody else. The number of executives who are unconsciously trying to prove themselves to their parents, either present or deceased, is mind-blowing. Their victories are hollow and very temporary. Well, let's put an end to that way of thinking right now. The name of the game is self-remembering not just self-improvement.

I often suggest to leaders that they get an index card, keep it in their wallet or purse, or even better make it their phone's wallpaper, and write these three simple words.

> *I am enough.*

These words, if said often enough, especially while looking in the mirror and saying them out loud, can change your life.

You have all the brilliance you need to shine already inside of you, just as the acorn has everything already within to be a grand oak tree, providing shade for generations to come. You simply need to add the pressure of nature, such as sunlight and patience. The acorn will do its bit—it has to, because it's a universal law.

All that's required is to make a decision. Like the decision, Deborah, my wife, and I made about what school to send our children to. We looked at all the possibilities and then finally chose the one that aligned best with our personal values and beliefs.

It was Redlands in Sydney Australia, and their school motto is "Let your light shine." Read those words again and say them out loud. How do they make you feel? Let—that's it, allow it, surrender to it, yield to the universal power that made you what you are. Your—your light, no one else's; not your parents', your teachers', or your CEO's. Yours. Light—you come into the world with unique talents to serve you and the world; this is your light. Shine—not just flicker, but truly shine. Your light is your gift to the world. "Let it shine, let it shine, let it shine." That's the decision you need to make right now: to find your light and then let it shine.

The problem is that after a while, if you're not careful, you can easily lose your lustre. You become a flicker, not a flame. It's too dark to find your way. Well, that's exactly what this book is all about: helping you find or rekindle your lustre. It's about polishing your own leadership diamond so brilliantly that you can't help but light up your room, your family, your team, your business, and the world.

But there's a big problem. Sometimes it appears too complicated to get there. As I go about my work, I come across all sorts of leadership capability or competency models. Some are simple and elegant. Some are disastrous. Some you'd never remember in a month of Sundays with over 160 "priority" competencies. They're kidding, aren't they? Did you know that originally the word *priority* was singular? We didn't have priorities. And even if you could remember 160 competencies, how would you ever get around to doing them?

In Marshall Goldsmith's Stakeholder Centric Coaching (based on *What Got You Here, Won't Get You There* and *Triggers*, which we've integrated into our work at *the human enterprise*), he suggests you pick one or two key growth areas and work on them for a whole year. Yes, that's right: one or two. The results are outstanding. It's all about priority and focus.

My point is that most leaders have little hope of having these competencies remain in their consciousness at all times. They become far too complex, far too overwhelming. That's where *Your Leadership Diamond* comes in. We know you can easily handle seven facets, and so we've done just that. We've isolated seven areas for you to focus on, to polish, to give real lustre to your leadership.

Easy, simple, memorable, and powerful. Just as diamonds have facets or faces to the world, so do you as a leader. Unless all those facets are truly shining, you'll never bring your light to the world in the way in which you're capable. Leave off a facet or fail to polish it, and the full lustre will never be there, bringing its sparkle to our world. As you polish one facet, you can't help but polish another. There are seven major facets of *Your Leadership Diamond* that you need to polish, and there's a key principle for each.

As simple as this model is, I can guarantee that from a long list of leadership competencies that many organisations insist their leaders learn, almost 90 per cent will fit under these seven simple facets. They're simple but not simplistic.

Here are the seven facets and the "polish principle" for each one:

LEADERSHIP FACET	POLISH PRINCIPLE
FACET 1: LEADING SELF	Raise your CONSCIOUSNESS.
FACET 2: LEADING ONE ON ONE	Make real CONNECTIONS.
FACET 3: LEADING TEAMS	Inspire collective COMMITMENT.
FACET 4: LEADING CLIENTS	Demonstrate heartfelt CARING.
FACET 5: LEADING THE ORGANISATION	Foster seamless COLLABORATION.
FACET 6: LEADING FAMILY & FRIENDS	Be their CHAMPION.
FACET 7: LEADING COMMUNITY	Honour your CALLING.

Throughout this book, I share seven specific techniques that align with these principles. There are many more techniques (in fact, at last count we have 112 of them at *the human enterprise*), yet I've chosen these ones not because they are the easiest to implement but because of their ability to really have you shine in a short space of time: seven weeks, or forty-nine days.

See yourself as a diamond, embrace the principles, and learn the techniques. There's one for you personally, four that are organisationally based, and two for your leadership outside of work. For each facet, there is a particular principle. These principles hold true for every technique no matter what. But you can't do a principle. For each of the seven facets, there are specific techniques, ideas that need to be implemented. Each action builds on the other, as you'll see in your seven-week programme. In fact, simply remembering the seven polish principles, in and of itself, will enhance your leadership effectiveness.

Let's look at each facet and see why it is so vital to your leadership success. The skills, techniques, and ideas will come later.

FACET 1: LEADING SELF -
RAISE YOUR CONSCIOUSNESS

As a leader, your role is to help your organisation reach its goals and simultaneously help individuals reach their own. As a leader, irrespective of your role in the business, growth has to be very high on your agenda. But let's look at where that growth really comes from. Again, organisations don't perform. People behave.

One of your key roles as a leader is to get people to change their behaviours, starting with your own. The genesis of all great behavioural change is self-awareness. You can't change what you're not aware of.

If you begin each day with the intention of becoming more aware of yourself, you'll begin to change. It'll be subtly and slowly at times, but you will change. The buzzword these days is mindfulness.

Every morning, set an intention for yourself as to who you wish to "be" that day: more assertive, more compassionate, more innovative, more relaxed, more confident, more humble, or whatever. Turn that into a specific set of behaviours. Your rituals. Then pay attention. Attention follows intention.

Monitor your daily habits, from the way you greet people of a morning, to the way you start and finish meetings, to the way you manage time, to your energy levels throughout the day. Pay attention to whatever will make a difference in achieving your intention. Be more mindful. Start the way you want to finish. Because in times of chaos, when the world seems out of control you can still take control of your own behaviour. Rituals put you in the driver's seat, irrespective of the uncertainties that surround you.

Leadership development really is an inside-out job. It starts with you being more aware. If you want to be a better leader, then you need to be a better you.

In Facet 1 I'll give you the most simple and profound way to do this. Your inspired awareness will take you to a whole new level.

FACET 2: LEADING ONE ON ONE -
MAKE REAL CONNECTIONS

The quality of your leadership is about the quality of your relationships. As Professors Goffee and Jones from London Business School say, leadership is a relationship.

The quality of your relationships is dependent upon the quality and quantity of the conversations you have with your people. I'm talking about all sorts of conversations: long ones, short ones, and ones in the corridor. Conversations about direction, how they can contribute, their talents, their needs, their skills, their skill gaps, their aspirations, and their personal goals and dreams. So many conversations during the year. Yet the key to all of these conversations—the basis of all great conversations and great relationships—is mutual trust and respect. It's not just getting them to trust you; it's also getting them to trust themselves.

Trust that they'll have the courage to put the real issues on the table, and trust that you'll listen without fear of retribution. The truth shall set you free.

Trust doesn't happen overnight. Sure, sometimes people will grant you immediate trust as their leader, but that's rare. Irrespective of your title, you have to earn it. One of the best ways of earning that trust is to make real connections with your associates. That means telling it how it is—the good, the bad, and the ugly, yet mostly the good. The technique you will learn in this facet says so much about you as a leader.

It says you're watching, it says you care, and it says they count, that their personal efforts are significant. It's one of the easiest and most powerful ways to bring to life.

FACET 3: LEADING TEAMS -
INSPIRE COLLECTIVE COMMITMENT

As great as it is to have strong relationships with individuals, it's the power of the team that counts and the commitment your team has to each other—not just to you, and not just to the mission, vision, or strategy, but to each other. In *Our Best*, a team focused Leadership Development Programme from *the human enterprise*, I talk about the four key ingredients that make up a high-performance team. It's what younger generations would call fully SICC. No, it's not a spelling mistake. It stands for:

Shared Purpose: crystal clarity on where we are going, our mission, our vision of greatness.

Interdependence: absolute surety around the way we need to work with each other, our ground rules, our protocols, our boundaries.

Commitment to the functional or sectional goals: Brilliantly implement these goals as well as the goals of each individual team member.

Commitment to each other as people: we should care about not just achieving team goals but individuals achieving their own personal ambitions.

For me, it's this last *C* that's the key. If you can get your individual team members totally committed to the success of each other, to have each other's backs, to genuinely yearn for their success, then just about everything else will fall into place. Anything can be accomplished.

On the surface, you'd think that having a fully SICC team would be easy. Ask most leaders, and they will tell you a very different story. They'll tell you how they have no trouble with Sharon or Peter personally, as individuals; it's just the way they work with the team that causes them angst. So in many ways, you are like a theatre director. You have all this talent that, left to its own devices, may become divisive. Your job is to bring these individuals cohesively together as a team. As in a theatre performance, they need to not only know their own lines but also have a solid understanding of the lines of the other performers. Why? To put on the play in the shortest time possible to the absolute delight of the audience—in your case, your customers.

This will involve conflict. If you're leading well, it will be constructive conflict; if not, relationships will be fragmented, and decisions will be far from optimal.

To achieve this, you have to really have your team connect with each other. They must realise their collective power and the joy and achievement that comes from true collaboration and shared expectations.

In Facet 3 I'll give you a simple and profound process to do this.

FACET 4: LEADING CLIENTS -
DEMONSTRATE HEARTFELT CARING

Every leader has clients, either internal or external. Some even go so far as to say that their direct reports are their clients. This is especially true if you have the philosophy that Robert Greenleaf recommends in *Servant Leadership* (and mentioned earlier in chapter 1), where every leader is primarily a steward of those in their care. As Richard Branson says "Clients do not come first. Employees come first. If you take care of your employees, they will take care of the clients."

There are thousands of books on customer service and hundreds of models. And there are thousands of people all around the planet who are attending customer service workshops as you read this book. They will be taught rapport-building skills, questioning skills (open and closed, of course), handling objections, and maybe even closing techniques. But that's only a start.

I'm not saying skills aren't important. But skills for the sake of skills, for the sake of getting the sale? No way. How shallow, how meaningless. We can get so hung up on the skill that we forget what's really important: Again, we marry the techniques and divorce the outcomes.

The greatest thing you can do for any customer is to truly, genuinely care. Care about their issues, their problems, their challenges, and their organisational context. Care about them personally. See them as people, not someone to whom you can sell something. Forget about the sale. Yes, if you forget about the sale and are truly there as a trusted adviser, then nine times out of ten, you'll end up with it anyway.

In this facet of *Your Leadership Diamond*, we overview four different levels of needs every client has and how to graciously meet them. It's not because it's a great technique but because you genuinely want to help, find out what's important in their world, and move them ahead in that world.

Focusing on this facet, will help you rekindle your love of customer service and the joy of truly serving. Your customers will get it. They'll see it in your every movement, hear it in your words, and feel it in their hearts, not just their heads.

That's why this part of the business is Facet 4.

FACET 5: LEADING THE ORGANISATION -
FOSTER SEAMLESS COLLABORATION

Irrespective of your title or level, in order to excel as a leader, you have to be proactive, thinking about and implementing organisational change. Dr Ichak Adizes, in his ground-breaking book *Mastering Change,* says that managing change (or disruption as it's now often referred to) is the role of a leader. Problems come from changes. Solutions are the answers to problems. But of course, new solutions bring a new set of problems. Therefore, leaders are primarily managers of change.

Nothing will get you promoted faster than developing a reputation as an organisational change agent, a leader of change. Notice that I said organisational, not just functional or team change agent.

Senior leaders absolutely love those who, without prompting, are constantly looking around to make things better.

As our world gets faster and faster, and as our customers become more demanding, and as things get harder, the natural default is to stick to your patch, your function, your section, your team. We hunker down, and the left hand won't know what the right hand is doing.

If that's the case, we never tap into the collective consciousness, the collective wisdom of the whole organisation. Solutions can become piecemeal, and a solution in one area without consultation can show up in another as a problem. We upset people, we have "patch" fights, we become even more narrow in our thinking, more siloed in our behaviour, and the exponential growth that's possible (the breakthroughs, the innovations) never occurs.

It doesn't have to be that way.

Your role is to get everyone seeing the bigger picture, to have everyone seeing that they are part of a larger plan, a whole system, in which each moving part impacts other moving parts in the system. Context is king.

You are one of those parts.

This doesn't have to be through big, organisational change projects. It's the little things that also bring us together and make us feel part of and connected to a large community. It's amazing how identifying, prioritising, and solving even the so-called small issues can rapidly transform your organisation.

The technique we'll be looking at for this facet is a way of thinking about organisations, followed by a series of questions.

You can ask these questions in every one on one interaction, every meeting, and every chance you get for personal reflection. Start thinking this way, and your impact on the total business will be outstanding. It's all done with a minimum of fuss. That's why the last of the organisational facets is Facet 5.

FACET 6: LEADING FAMILY AND FRIENDS -
BE THEIR CHAMPION

There is immense joy and sadness in the work I do as a transformational leadership coach. Part of that is getting leaders to see that they are so much more than just their job titles. I help extend their identity well beyond business. When this happens, they are unstoppable, take great strength from the nurturing of family and friends, and become more balanced, energised, and effective leaders. Their energy goes out to excite followers to exceptional performance. That's pure joy for me.

But sadly, this doesn't always happen. There are so many demands on a leader these days that your time never seems to be your own. Therefore, you often make commitments to everyone who asks, hoping and praying that the workload is just temporary, that it will lessen, that it will go away. It never does.

We deny ourselves time with the people for whom we are doing all of this. The ones who love us, the ones who will be there for us long after last month's figures have been analysed to death, long after the settling of the new restructure or the recent merger. Long after the relationships from work may seem a distant memory, the regret of not being there physically, emotionally, and spiritually for the family will still linger.

As I mentioned in the preface, I have experienced my own regrets when, as primarily an international trainer, I spent too many days away from home. Of course, the real sad thing is that in many ways, it's family you're doing all this for in the first place. Don't forget that.

Yes, it's tough to get the balance right. None of us are saints, but in this facet of *Your Leadership Diamond,* we'll be overviewing some simple ideas that just say one thing: "I love you. I care." That is often all you need to remember with Facet 6.

FACET 7: LEADING COMMUNITY -
HONOUR YOUR CALLING

I've met very few great leaders who don't want to give back in some way and want to play a bigger game. They get the importance of success but want to also move to significance and make a real difference in the world. As one leader told me, "There'll always be a bigger boat." The great leaders want to leave their mark on the world, or as Steve Jobs said, "a dent in the universe." That universe could be global, or it could be your local school. It's still a dent.

I recently spent time with the wife of an international hairdresser who has 50 hairdressing salons throughout the world and 350 team members. I commented that her husband must be very proud of what he has achieved in business. She agreed but also added he is proudest of what he has done for the industry and the lives of the people his creativity has touched. By globally raising the professional status of hairdressers, he's given a massive dose of self-esteem to so many, as well as hope and inspiration. He's replicated this formula around the world—the ultimate rinse and repeat.

He is taking people to a better place. For this, he was given a form of knighthood in Holland. What will your life stand for?

What will your legacy be?
Who will you leave your mark on?

We're all going to cry when we're born. How many will cry for us when we make our ultimate departure? And not because they're grieving for your loss, but they cry tears of joy for having known you and having been touched by your kindness, your compassion, your never-ending faith in them, and the difference you made in their world?

I don't know exactly what your calling is, but I know you have one. If you can combine this calling with what the world truly needs, you'll be unstoppable. You can wait passively until you receive some message from on high. You can learn more and more about yourself, your values, your beliefs, and your karmic destiny. Or you can simply go out and start doing some good in the world. There will never be a right time or a better time than now. Make that time. That time is now. You have a calling, as I point out in Facet 7.

Now that you know the facets of *Your Leadership Diamond* and the key principle for each, here's a glimpse of the specific technique you'll be polishing for each facet.

"YOUR LEADERSHIP DIAMOND"

DIAMOND FACET	KEY PRINCIPLE	SPECIFIC TECHNIQUE
1. Leading SELF	Raise your CONSCIOUSNESS.	Be Present.
2. Leading ONE ON ONE	Make real CONNECTIONS.	Give Credits.
3. Leading TEAMS	Inspire collective COMMITMENT.	Set Ground Rules.
4. Leading CLIENTS	Demonstrate heartfelt CARING.	Exceed Needs.
5. Leading THE ORGANISATION	Foster seamless COLLABORATION.	Think Whole Systems.
6. Leading FAMILY & FRIENDS	Be their CHAMPION.	Show Up.
7. Leading COMMUNITY	Honour your CALLING.	Get Involved.

PART 2
THE FACETS

FACET 1: LEADING SELF
RAISE YOUR CONSCIOUSNESS

In an earlier life, I had two psychology clinics in Sydney. When working with individuals who were having relationship difficulties, I detected two subtle but important patterns, one of which was right in front of me.

The first pattern was that in reviewing their pasts, many often found it difficult to remember that much detail. Second, when they were trying to explain past relationships, they were everywhere—fidgeting, looking around the office, focusing on anything but me. And the reason? They simply weren't present. They were not present to me at that moment, not present in their past. That was why their memories were so bland.

We're all old enough to realise there is no one secret to having a great life, but there probably is one secret to great leadership when it comes to relationships. Be present. Nothing increases mutual trust and respect like being present. In order to do this, you have to raise your consciousness about being present in the first place.

How many managers do you know who are with you physically but not mentally, and certainly not emotionally? They're somewhere else, anywhere but with you. Sure, they'll nod and go through the motions, but it's difficult to believe they really want to be with you when they:

- Don't make eye contact
- Finish your sentences for you
- Never paraphrase
- Answer their mobiles
- Check their texts
- Say hello to everyone who passes
- Play with papers on their desks

And that's just the beginning. My beautiful mate, Steve (whom I mentioned earlier), says they're not distracted; they're simply "attracted" to something else that appears more important or exciting at the time than being with you. But how does that make you feel? Is it just a lack of attention?

Attention Deficit Syndrome (ADS) gets a lot of press these days, particularly with children, although the latest research is showing it's prevalent in adults as well. But again, Steve suggested to me that leaders who appear to not be present lack not attention but intention. You could say that many leaders have Intention Deficit Syndrome (IDS). Make it your clear intention to be truly present to whomever you're with.

> *"Love the one you're with."*
> Stephen Stills

You can easily forget that right now, the person that you're speaking with is where your focus should be. All the skills in the world (one of which we will look at in "Leading

One on One") will mean zip, nada, nothing if you're not truly connecting with the person in front of you.

Amongst the Zulus of the northern Natal tribes of South Africa, the word for *hello* is Sawubona, which means "I see you." How great is that? It's not just an off-the-cuff hi; it's really seeing people, making them feel significant, important. They know that they count.

But get this: the reply is even more revealing. It's "Ngikhona," which means "I am here." Wow, I exist only after you have acknowledged that you see me. In fact, your saying hello to me brings me into existence. The sophistication of these greetings is inspiring.

In order to bring yourself to the present and raise your consciousness, embrace these three most important questions and their answers.

- What is the most important time in life?
  Right now (the present).
- What is the most important thing in life?
  What you're doing right now.
- Who is the most important person in the world?
  The person right in front of you.

So how do you get present?

FOUR KEYS

People do this in their own way. Here are some tried and tested strategies.

1. **Make it your intention to get present to both yourself and others.**

   As simple as it is, make it your intention to be fully present to whoever you're with. A mantra, or saying to yourself, is a good reminder or trigger: "Be here," or "Get present," or even "Pay attention."

   This means putting aside your own ideas and agenda and truly listening to what others are saying for every one on one, every phone call, every meeting. And of course, getting present to your body through the power of three big breaths is a classic strategy. Why? Because it works.

2. **Give them your attention.**

   This means making more eye contact than you normally would and getting rid of distractions (e.g., your mobile, iPad, or diary). See the person's "magnificence," assuming positive intent about their actions and words. Calm and stop the internal chatter in your own mind.

3. **Truly focus on someone as a person.**

   Buddhists say every time we meet someone, there is a chance to teach or a chance to learn. See the person in front of you as someone who either has a lesson or a message for you, or someone whom you can teach, help, or develop on his or her journey. By doing this you'll be much more focused on who they are, what they're saying, and what you're hearing. You'll be fully appreciating who they are and their message.

4. **Show up with an open mind.**
   So often we lose our presence because we come with prepared answers to the issues we are about to discuss. We are listening for other people's "rightness," the degree to which they are in alignment (or not) to our way of thinking or our agenda. We listen through our own filters.

It's like there are four buttons that simultaneously need to be pressed in order to be present.

RAISING YOUR CONSCIOUSNESS

INTENTION is	ON	Deliberately being present.
ATTENTION is	OUT	Not on you but them.
APPRECIATION is	UP	Of them as a person.
AGENDA is	OFF	Being fully open to possibilities.

Raising your consciousness by being fully present is also at the heart of most great performers. By being fully present, you develop an extraordinary amount of self-awareness, the genesis of all great learning. Nick O'Hern, in his golf book *Tour Mentality: Inside the Mind of a Golf Pro,* sums it up beautifully when he states the key to great shot making is "stay in the present, commit to the process." It's time to raise your consciousness, time to push your buttons.

ON A PERSONAL NOTE

As I discussed, for many years my daughter, Ruby, suffered from epileptic seizures. As her dad, all I wanted to do was to make it better for her, to take away her pain and the embarrassment she often experienced. I always listened to her through a filter or lens of "I've got to come up with a solution here. For God's sake, I'm her dad."

I was Mr Positive:
"We'll get this cured."
"This will work out. You'll see."
"Together we will find a way."

Yet Ruby got sicker and sicker. One night I sat on her bed, listening to her account of her seizures that day. No solutions, no rah-rah, no "we can do it." I simply listened. And for the first time, I really understood what it was like to be in her world—the fear, the uncertainty, the struggle, the humiliation, the sadness.

I'd always been the strong one, yet as I sat there and truly listened, tears poured down my face. Ruby wiped them away, told me to cheer up, and hugged me. We both went off to sleep. The next morning, I awoke to find on my bedside table the most beautiful drawing of the Little Mermaid. Ruby's artistic skills were awe-inspiring. On the picture was this simple note: "Dear Dad, thank you so much for our loving conversation last night." It's one of my most precious possessions.

Sometimes just being truly present is the greatest gift you can give to the world. And as a leader, it's the greatest gift you can give your people.

> *"Wherever you are, be there."*
> Jim Rohn

TIME FOR REFLECTION

What is it that causes you not to be present to yourself? In not being with yourself, you are not being present to others. Why do we make the choice to be distracted, to go this way or that? Do those choices really matter?

I often think that for me, it's that I don't want to miss out on anything. The appeal of the new bright, shiny object is greater than the pull of being truly present to myself and others. I allow myself to be distracted because I don't want to miss out.

So what's with the fear of missing out, or FOMO as people say? I believe it's because we so much want to be in the know, to not be found lacking or wanting. By being in the know, we will be more acceptable to others, more appealing, more loveable. Yet if this is what our souls are really craving— real connection—isn't it amazing that the opportunity for connection is in front of you right now? Getting present to yourself will reveal so much. It's like looking into a still pond and seeing your reflection, your true self, for the first time. But if you keep throwing bright, shiny objects into the pond, all you'll do is create ripples, and your self-image will be distorted. You will never be clear.

What if rather than going from one thing to another seeking joy and happiness, you sucked the marrow and joy out of the present? For the more commercially minded, it's like investor Warren Buffet buying a small portion of shares after careful analysis and then really getting the best out of those shares (in our case, the moments). It's putting all your eggs in one basket and then really watching that basket.

The alternative is buying lots of shares, skipping across the surface, and selling them on a whim or a hot tip from your Uber driver to buy something different. Not only is it exhausting, it's probably not the path to real financial wealth or gaining those feelings of abundance in your life.

Learn to focus and to be grateful for what's in front of you, for what you have in your life, for a still pond.

FIRST WEEK: SMALL TWEAK 1

Make it your intention to be aware of your attention. Push those four buttons: ON, OUT, UP and OFF. Make a concerted effort at least once a day to make eye contact and truly be with the person in front of you. You'll find after your first week of getting more present to yourself, others, and your environment, you'll feel more grounded, more real, more honest, more whole, and more authentic. This raised level of mindfulness will begin to flow into all your relationships with others and the physical world. It seems so simple and almost uneventful. Let me assure you that it's one of the most powerful things you can do as a leader. Now you're ready to polish the second facet of *Your Leadership Diamond*, "Leading One on One."

FACET 2: LEADING ONE ON ONE
MAKE REAL CONNECTIONS

It's vital for leaders to make real connections with their team, their peers, their bosses, their suppliers, and of course, their customers (both external and internal). Often leaders come to me wanting to do a "team" workshop, and they ask me what they can do in the meantime to help the team. I give them the answer in three words: one on ones.

The team works in direct proportion to the quality of the relationships you have with every individual on the team. The best one on one skill—and yes, it is a skill—is to credit and recognise the performances of others.

There's a certain mindset associated with your ability to give credit. First of all, you have to be looking for what works, not what isn't working. Psychologists call it appreciative inquiry.

Second, you must have, as they say in personal development circles, an attitude of gratitude. You have to appreciate the players in your life and what they do to help you move forward in your world.

Finally, you have to decide whether you are going to be a diminisher or a multiplier in every interaction. Multipliers leave people, places, and projects so much better than when they found them.

One of those places is your home. There's an old saying when people get up to tricks and pranks: "Don't try this at home." But that's exactly what I do want you to do with this second facet of *Your Leadership Diamond*. If we can't give heartfelt gratitude to family and friends, to whom can we give it?

Now that you're so present to people (Facet 1) and are actively looking for opportunities to credit, not criticise, you'll see a shift in your own energy and the energy of those around you. This one technique will make a massive difference in your life and the lives of others. I can promise you that it can change your whole outlook on life. Don't wait until you feel better about your team or peers—do it now, and you'll immediately feel better.

> *"The bird doesn't sing because it has an answer,*
> *it sings because it has a song."*
> Maya Angelou

There are so many skills vital to learn in this facet of *Your Leadership Diamond*. It's where many new leaders, who have been great technicians and promoted because of their technical skills, struggle.

In our leadership development programmes and one on one coaching, irrespective of the seniority of the leaders, we often look at delegation skills, coaching skills, mediation skills, conflict-resolution skills, training skills, and constructive feedback skills. All of these are vital for any leader to know and to do well. But my favourite is crediting and recognition skills. In psychology, this is often called positive reinforcement. It's the old behavioural maxim that any behaviours reinforced in the present increases the chances of it being repeated in the future.

To me, it's the most powerful leadership skill on the planet. It makes you feel great and improves both the performance and the self-esteem bank (as Stephen Covey called it in *The 7 Habits of Highly Effective People*) of the person you are crediting. I call it the Force. Obviously, it's a play on words from the *Star Wars* movies. I like to imagine the original line in the movie was going to be, "Let the positive reinFORCEment be with you," but they cut it down to "May the force be with you" for impact.

WHAT IS A CREDIT?

A credit is many things. But what's often overlooked is that a credit is performance-related feedback. It's answering the key questions every team member craves: "How am I doing? Am I seen as an individual? Am I seen as part of a tribe? How do I contribute? Am I significant? Am I valued?"

You see, it's not just fluffy compliments. If you're old enough to remember Mr Grace in *Are You Being Served?* he used to say, "You've all done very, very well." What made this funny is that it's too close to the bone. He was the elderly owner of the business who didn't know what was happening on the shop floor. But complimenting isn't crediting.

Don't get me wrong. What Mr Grace does is better than no feedback at all. But here's the trouble. When you simply say "good job," "well done," or "great effort," it's just a compliment. It's not a leadership credit. As you'll see in a moment, a leadership credit goes well beyond that. A leadership credit is a very specific, four-part tool, with each step being an essential psychological building block.

What's often revealing in our leadership development programmes is when participants get 360-degree feedback that says that their stakeholders believe they don't credit them, yet the participants swear that they do.

The problem is this that they are complimenting them, not crediting them. They are recognising them, not appreciating them. More on this in a minute. For now, let's look at the specific parts of a credit. But before we do, let's look at what's at the heart of crediting.

Focusing on what works in an organisational context is, as we said, what we call appreciative inquiry. It's appreciating and asking questions on what works rather than focussing only on problems or issues. In terms of leading one on one, we call it crediting, or building the self-esteem bank of the people with whom you work.

Imagine that the people in your team are banks, and they're filled with either lots of or not many self-esteem chips. As Stephen Covey says in his book *The 7 Habits of Highly Effective People*, your job is to build people's self-esteem banks. Increase the number of deposits. Do it in a genuine, positive, and sincere way. Do it by focusing on what they do well. Place a token into their self-esteem bank. Make them feel good about themselves. Do it because people who feel good about themselves produce good results, as Blanchard tells us in *The One Minute Manager*.

Some of your people will have huge self-esteem chips in their accounts, and others will be almost bankrupt for all sorts of reasons. If you want people to take risks and innovate, you have to build up their self-esteem accounts long before you ask them to do anything.

I believe people actually like change. What they don't like are the possibilities change brings, especially the possibility of failure. They don't like to fail because they're afraid they won't be able to bounce back. You have to build resilience. You have to exercise the courage muscle. You have to make sure no matter what happens, people have enough self-esteem in their account to master any changes. That's the job of a leader.

WHEN DO YOU CREDIT?

You make a credit when:

- *Someone exceeds a standard.* These people stand out very easily; they're the high performers in the business, and they often get a lot of accolades.
- *Someone constantly meets the standard.* These people probably don't scream out, but they're constantly there, always doing the right thing and always on the money. These people often don't get any feedback and float the possibility of leaving. Only at that point do we say, "Don't leave. You're one of our best people." Pay attention to the people who are constantly meeting standards.
- *People meet an outcome or standard not normally met by them.* In other words, someone has done something major she normally wouldn't do. Someone has finally learned the process and has put a little more effort than normal. Your job as a leader is to catch her at that point in terms of going beyond a standard she normally doesn't reach, or an effort she normally doesn't show.

THE FOUR STEPS OF CREDITING

We have a pneumonic for this called USSR. It's based on a line from the Beatles song *Back in the USSR,* when they say, "You don't know how lucky you are, boy. Back in the USSR." It's a reminder to be grateful for the people around you.

U—the first step of crediting is an *upfront,*
    positive general reference
S—the second step is a *specific* example
S—the third step is a *skill* or quality
R—the final one is a *resulting benefit*

U.S.S.R.

I mentioned beforehand that when we do organisational surveys, we often speak to leaders who say, "Yes, I'm giving my people credits all the time." Again, what they don't realise is they're giving them compliments, not credits.

Suppose that your team does a particularly great presentation. You could say, "Great presentation. That was fantastic." Again, that is a compliment, not a credit. It doesn't give them any feedback about themselves, and neither does it tell them how that presentation actually helped.

Let's have a look in more detail.

- **Upfront, positive general reference:** first, you say, "That was a brilliant presentation you did yesterday," to the marketing department. Notice that it's a general reference to what's been said (the presentation), and it's an upfront positive (brilliant).
- **Specific:** the second step is a specific example of what they did well. "Hey, the way you took the brand into account and linked it to the supply chain showed a fantastic example of what real partnership is about." Notice how I've shown that I do pay attention, and I've let them know what I specifically appreciate.
- **Skill or quality:** but here comes the most important part of a credit. When you do this, you credit the person, not just what they did. You credit the skill or quality they used to do it. "I was particularly impressed with the initiative you took." Notice how it says something about the person, not what they did.
- **Resulting benefit:** the final step is to link the credit back to organisational performance, objectives, higher purpose, and mission. "As a result, the marketing department has agreed to what we've said, and it's going to get our product launched into the marketplace a lot sooner."

The team now knows how they fit in. We've let them know that what they do counts and has meaning. If there's one thing people are looking for, it's meaning. A great way of showing people how they fit in, and how what they do counts, is to show the connection between what they're working on and a higher purpose.

There's a story that beautifully reinforces this, and yes, it's been around a long time. It's about someone walking onto a building site. He comes across the first bricklayer and says, "What are you doing?" The answer is, "I'm laying bricks." He seems a bit lethargic.

He comes across the next bricklayer, asks the same question, and receives this response: "Actually, I'm building a wall. It's a great building." Note that he feels more part of it.

He then comes across a third bricklayer, and this time the quality's higher, but what strikes the questioner is that this bricklayer is ecstatic. He asks him, "What are you doing?"

He replies, "Man, I'm building the best sanctuary for homeless kids they will ever have." Notice how for the final bricklayer, it's not just a job. It's linked to a higher purpose. That's what we do with the skill of crediting. Try it. It works!

I had a neighbour who used to come out with his kids on a Sunday with a Zero Weeding Brush and some tools to pick out the weeds in his lawn. That always struck me as quite weird because he was focusing on the weeds. On the other hand, I had read a comment in a gardening book with a different approach. It suggested that if you aerate the lawn (I use my old golf shoes with metal spikes to do this) and then water and fertilise it, the lawn becomes so lush that it pops out the weeds.

You have to come to a decision in your own mind: are you a weeder or are you a lawner? Are you going to focus on what's wrong (the weeds) or on what's right and the solutions? I suggest you focus on the lawn. Will you have weeds? Absolutely, but you're more easily able to deal with them. If not, you'll be picking out weeds for the rest of your life.

But why do so many leaders do so poorly on engagement surveys in this area, particularly when they think giving recognition is one of their strengths? There are many reasons for this. A key one is they have not made the distinction between recognition and appreciation.

They recognise the tasks that people do and even the outcomes, but they fail to appreciate them as people who are making a real impact, letting them know their contribution counts. This is why I believe the most important part of crediting is appreciating the people, not simply recognising the task. More than anything, this builds their self-esteem bank. It makes them feel truly valued for who they are, not just for what they did. As a leader, you have a duty, an obligation, a responsibility to help everyone you touch grow. To be the best they can be. You must remember you may be the only person in your associate's life that's ever believed in them.

You can now see the importance of each individual steps of USSR. All the steps have a significant part to play in crediting. I assure you this will be the most important skill you'll ever learn as a leader. "Trust the force."

STEPS		PART THEY PLAY
Upfront Positive General Reference	WHEN	Gives context and lets the performer know "hey something good is coming down the line."
Specific Examples	WHAT	Makes it real, says "i'm watching you, i care." Gives authenticity and sincerity. Shows how great work gets recognised.
Skill or Quality	WHO	Let's them know that they count. It's who they are that counts not just what they did. Appreciates them as a person.
Resulting Benefits	WHY	Let's them know how they fit into the bigger picture. How they help achieve the Vision, align with Higher Purpose; or just how they help themselves, peers, customers, suppliers and the community.

ON A PERSONAL NOTE

Most people have a bucket list, or a list of things they'd love to do before they "kick the bucket." We really need a better term than this, but this one's so familiar.

Let's call it your lifetime list. On mine, I had to run a marathon. Yes, 26.2 miles, or 41.8 kilometres. I was never that fast at school, but I had a very low heart rate (I still do). For some reason, I could run forever, and I represented the district in cross-country. But of course, the ultimate test of that is a marathon.

In August 1984, I entered the inaugural Sydney Wang Marathon. (Wang was one of the original word-processing companies.) I was working for CIG (now BOC) at the time and saw one of our engineering managers in the crowd who had recently resigned. He was one of those amazingly fit characters, the type who's always running at lunchtime and full of smiles and energy. Sadly, I can't even remember his name, but I'll never forget the difference he made to my life that day.

Frankly, I wasn't super fit, but I was amazingly determined. Off I went, and like Forrest Gump, I kept running. After talking with a few veterans earlier, they'd suggested not to put too much pressure on myself and to simply make it my goal to finish. But that didn't quite cut it with me. I wanted some goal, some target. I thought ten kilometres an hour was a fair pace to do—in fact a smidge more than this—and so I set myself a goal of four hours.

Now, I was young, reasonably fit, and motivated, but at forty kilometres I was spent, absolutely stuffed. I set myself four more mini goals. "Just do another five hundred metres, then another, then another," until I'd reached the finish line. At 41.5 kilometres, I'd reached the stadium. Only three hundred metres, not even a full lap, to finish. But as soon as I entered, I froze like a deer in the headlights. Crazy as it is, I knew I had absolutely nothing left, and after all that work I would not finish the race. My legs weren't just aching—I couldn't even feel them. My whole body was totally dried out, like an old beach towel in the sun. I could not go on.

And then came this voice from the stands: the young engineering manager's voice. He must have finished much earlier. Somehow, I heard it above all the others. "Come on, Paul. You've come this far! You can do it! Don't give up, mate. Keep going, keep going!"

I lifted. Not by much mind you, but I lifted enough to see the big time clock at the finish. Where I got that last spurt of energy from, I'll never know, but I ran across the finish line and was given a time card: three hours, fifty-eight minutes. I never saw the engineer again; he was a nameless person in the crowd, just a casual acquaintance. Yet his words of encouragement got me across the line that day. Simple but powerful.

"Come on, Paul. You've come this far! You can do it! Don't give up, mate. Keep going, keep going!"

For some reason, those words are embedded in my soul. There have been so many times when I've been so low in life and about to throw in the towel, and then I remember those words of hope and encouragement. Now I try to be that voice for others.

And you are that voice in the crowd for so many as well. Perhaps you'll never know the difference your words of encouragement will mean to someone else. Perhaps you may never meet again, but never underestimate the power of the force. Never underestimate what your passionate support and encouragement can do to lift someone's performance, to lift someone's spirits. It's the ultimate connection to our humanity.

TIME FOR REFLECTION

It's so easy to outline the four key steps of USSR, to make the distinction between recognition and appreciation. So why don't we do it? That is, give credit where credit is due.

Let's explore this for a minute. Do you think you credit enough, too much, or hardly at all? Like many leadership skills, I believe our relationship with crediting goes back to our family of origin when we were kids.

Think for a bit. What was crediting or acknowledging like in your family? Did you celebrate the opening of an envelope? Did everyone receive bundles and bundles of recognition in your family, or was it not there at all, or was it rationed out? The impact on your leadership will be huge.

Did other siblings get recognition, but not you? Or were you the bright, shining star and felt embarrassed by how much praise you got compared to your siblings? There are those families that feel any form of acknowledgement spoils a child. If that's your family of origin, then no matter what you did, it never seemed good enough. It's staggering the number of leaders I come across (mostly male) whose achievements are a way of showing their dads they're worthy and that they've made something of themselves.

Did you only get credit when you really achieved something of greatness, never for just your efforts? Then again, did your parents pour it on so that you got a certificate for simply getting out of bed of a morning? All of this will impact your willingness, awareness, and skill in crediting. Reflect on the why of past crediting and then ask yourself how you wish to credit going forward. How do you now wish to excite others to exceptional performance? To acknowledge outcomes and efforts? To not just recognise what they did but also appreciate who they are?

SECOND WEEK: SMALL TWEAK 2

Now you're mindful of being present. Because of this, you have a growing awareness of the contributions people are making in your world. You're seeing credit candidates everywhere. Your words of encouragement are lifting not only other people's spirits and performances but yours as well. You've set yourself a goal. Give one genuine, full credit a day. At first it may seem like a big effort, but soon enough it will be the most rewarding part of your day. You're now ready to polish the third facet of *Your Leadership Diamond*, leading teams.

FACET 3: LEADING TEAMS
INSPIRE COLLECTIVE COMMITMENT

Here's a prediction I have for you. Many years from now, you may find yourself alone and thinking about the work you used to do. I can promise you with unbelievable certainty that you won't remember what the numbers were for the fourth quarter in 2030, or the growth rate or the EBIT, or any other measure.

No, if you're like most retired leaders I know, you'll be thinking about the people. The characters you met along the way. The relationships you forged. How when the team broke up after almost three years together, even though all were promotions, you still teared up.

You'll remember how you once dressed up as Santa at the work Christmas party and distributed presents to associates' kids; it was the best thing you did all year. Or how your "macho," type-A supply manager couldn't pass through his fears at that band camp when it came to the flying fox. Then he broke down and shared his vulnerabilities, and the whole team was so compassionate with him.

Or how a marketing peer was so tough on you, and her perfectionist behaviour went beyond a joke until she shared with you (after a few red wines) how deep down she felt she was a failure; all the perfectionist behaviour was just compensation, a cover-up.

This is what you'll remember. You'll remember the people, and you'll remember the relationships—some brilliant, some good, some bad, and some ugly. Relationships involve emotions, and emotions are stored in the long-term memory, the limbic system, well after the logic of the fourth-quarter figures are figments of your imagination. Humans are social beings unless they're a psychopath (no, don't give a copy to your boss with this bit highlighted). We have an inbuilt need to congregate, to collaborate, to connect, to form community.

At no time is this sense of community more needed than in times of crisis. Although many of us have an independent part, there's something in our DNA that tells us we will only get through the tough times if we band together. Our community or connecting part. Victor Frankl, in his classic book *Man's Search for Meaning*, tells us in graphic terms that the survivors of concentration camps in the Second World War all had something to live for. A relative, a place, a higher purpose, something of meaning. There is great comfort and meaning in community. And incredible energy.

I find again and again that the great leaders get this. They are great connectors, and they connect to you on much more than a functional level. They get you and the whole business connecting to a "higher purpose." They connect people to each other. They inspire collective commitment—which is not easy. No, the lure of hitting your own numbers, at looking after your own patch, your own silo, is very seductive.

Dr Barry Oshry tells us that systematically there is a constant struggle, between dispersion (doing your own thing) and integration as one team, particularly for middle managers.

This integration can happen at many altitudes, from simply sharing information or group problem-solving at base camp to summiting as a fully united climbing party or power bloc.

In Oshry's brilliant workshop "The Organisation Workshop: Creating Partnership across Boundaries," he also says, "We don't integrate because we think we have nothing in common. Whereas the truth is exactly the opposite. Because if we did integrate we'd realise just how much we have in common."

SO HOW DO YOU INTEGRATE? HOW DO YOU INSPIRE COLLECTIVE COMMITMENT?

In our programme "Our Best: Transforming Higher Performance Individuals into a High Performance Team," we help you implement a number of vital tools and processes.

- Getting to know each other's talents, needs, and vulnerabilities
- Genuinely getting it all out on the table—where it's working, where it's not, and where at times it's just a disaster
- Setting specific behavioural ground rules or a team charter (not just values)
- Looking at how decisions are made

- Agreeing on ways to respond to ideas that are put forward
- Exploring boundaries and expectations we have of each other
- Inspiring a collective personalised mission and legacy for the team that aligns with, but is different to, the organisational vision or purpose
- Seeing how we keep ourselves accountable

Now, let's focus on one of these tools, the setting of ground rules. Setting ground rules is committing to how we wish to be with each other as a team.

You may recall in an earlier chapter of this book, I summarised what each of the facets of *Your Leadership Diamond* were. Within this, I outlined the fully SICC model of high-performance teams.

- They all have a **S**hared Purpose (a focus on results)
- They all have absolute clarity around their **I**nterdependencies (shared accountabilities)
- They are all **C**ommitted to each other's functions (buy-in and commitment)
- And the real breakthrough; they are all **C**ommitted to each other's personal success (mutual trust and respect)

Here's an example of commitment to each other's personal success. I once worked with a team I that all knew they were going to be retrenched because their division was going to be closed down. Rather than feeling "helpless" and falling for the seduction of the blame game, they became helpful to each other. They made a commitment that irrespective of when they were eventually shut down, they would stay in touch and support each other until everyone in the team gained fulfilling re-employment. And they did.

COMMITTING TO EACH OTHER

There are many ingredients to baking a successful trust pie, yet one of the best I know is to have you and your team create a set of ground rules. Now, some don't like this term, so call it your living principles, your team charter, your team guidelines, your team code, or whatever you want. Simply remember the purpose is to get you all on the same page about the way you will work together. Manage expectations upfront. That way, there is constructive (not destructive) conflict. But how do you get on the same page?

Simon Sinek encourages us in his book *Start with WHY*. I agree that there's nothing more important than an inspiring a shared purpose, the why. But the inspiration will be short-lived if you don't work out exactly how you are going to be with each other along the way. How will you work together, what's expected, and what's not? What's tolerated and what's not? What's in scope and what's out?

I don't know where I first heard it, yet I love the expression "When there are no rules, people make up their own." Great management of individual teams, clients, friends, and family is about managing expectations. Many teams get into destructive conflict because they have never discussed and agreed how they will work together, which can sometimes be their undoing. By all means, start with your noble or higher purpose. But rather than going straight on to your team mission, first agree how you will connect. How will you not just tolerate but seek out and encourage constructive conflict in the team?

Let me let you into a secret. Even if you think your team doesn't have any ground rules, they do. They are there, they are tacit, they are unwritten, and they are unspoken—but they are there. The best thing you can do as a leader is to put them on the table. Bring them out into the open. Not acknowledging the unwritten ground rules is a recipe for disaster: *"If you can mention it, you can manage it."*

If not, people get hurt. They make up stories about one another in which they are mostly the victim about how someone in the team is not performing. The sad part is that the so-called non-performer probably doesn't even know what he is guilty of. It's never been discussed. It's never been made clear. We failed to put it on the table. While working with a very successful organisation in Asia, I asked the COO, "How come they are so much more successful than their competitors?" Quick as a flash, he answered, "Because we discuss the undiscussables."

Undiscussables have an energy about them. For example, everyone knows the boss is a control freak or is always late to her own meetings. It upsets the team, but no one says anything—well, not directly to the boss. It's an undiscussable. But let me assure you that if you're the boss, your behaviour is being discussed with the other team members, yet never in the open. It's pushed down, but that takes energy. And much like a beach ball being held down in a pool, when you eventually stop pushing it down, it will shoot out of the pool with amazing force. In my leadership shadow work, I say it eventually pops up with demonic energy.

The energy used to not discuss, to not mention, and to push things under the table is energy that detracts the team away from its purpose. Dr Ichak Adizes, from The Adizes Institute, illustrates this perfectly in his success formula.

$$\text{SUCCESS} = f \left\{ \frac{\overset{\text{Opportunities}}{\nwarrow} \quad \overset{\text{Capabilities}}{\nearrow}}{\text{External Integration}} \middle/ \frac{\text{Internal DISintegration}}{\underset{\text{Mutual Trust}}{\swarrow} \quad \underset{\text{Mutual Respect}}{\searrow}} \right\}$$

© Dr. Ichak Adizes

He sees success in personal and organisational life as an equation. It's a function of the numerator (the top number) being the amount of energy you have available for External Integration. In our case, it's how well you match your organisational capabilities to the opportunities and the needs of the marketplace.

However, it's not all smooth sailing. This number, and therefore the overall energy available and the success of the system, is divided by the denominator (the bottom figure), which is what Dr Adizes calls Internal DISintegration such as politics, unclear vision, mission or values, lack of role clarity, or doing business with yourself. Essentially, it's anything that erodes mutual trust and respect.

Energy is neither created nor destroyed and only goes to one place at a time, so where do you think it goes to first? Exactly! To internal disintegration. This must be reduced if your team and organisation have any hope of succeeding and fostering mutual trust and respect. Only then can you optimise the amount of energy available for your clients, the subject of our next chapter. Ground rules help you do just that.

In our team programmes, we point out how team members have a choice. They can play ping pong or put the bowling balls on "the table of truth."

A ping pong team is a low-performance team. They will simply pass light issues across the table all day long. Sure, there will be a few volleys and smashes, but we never mention the real issues. No one calls it.

> *"Don't mention the war."*
> Basil Fawlty

On the other hand, high-performance teams move towards the tension. If not, they know it will go underground and eventually end up biting them.

The bowling balls are all those things that are heavy to lift and may even put a dent in the table. But for real honesty, for real trust and mutual respect, they must be said. If not, your integrity, and that of the teams, suffers enormously. So the question is, how do you put the bowling balls on the table?

First of all, don't turn every issue into a bowling ball, and don't turn your team into an AMF bowling alley. All that causes is more drama.

When I was a kid, I was the goody two shoes in the family, and my brother was the absolute opposite. He was continually in trouble at school, though it was nothing serious and he never hurt anyone. Yet I can remember even for little misdemeanours, Mum used to say, "Colin, how could you? Wait till your father gets home." The tension would mount, and by the time Dad did get home, one could cut the air with a knife over what were really small issues. For starters, let a few of the smaller ones through to the keeper, as they say in cricket. But never do so continually.

Every time you let someone get away with a behaviour that doesn't help the team in the long run, you are subtly making it OK. Your lack of calling it is what makes it possible. We teach people how to treat us.

Again, the best way I know how to put the bowling ball on the table, to move towards the tension, is to have or nurture an environment that drives out fear and drives up trust. One of the best ways of doing that is for the team to co-create a set of ground rules or behaviours by which they all agree to live.

So how do you go about this?

STEPS TO CREATING TEAM GROUND RULES

1. Link them to organisational values.
2. Start where you are at.
3. Make them behaviourally specific.
4. Bring them to life.
5. Make them real.
6. Agree how to reinforce them.
7. Agree how to enforce them.

THE OVERALL FORMULA FOR SETTING GROUND RULES

Here it is, simple yet powerful. You simply have to fill in the blanks: We (ADVERB) (VERB) (VALUE) by (BEHAVIOUR).

For example: *We constantly (adverb) demonstrate (verb) respect (value) by being on time for all meetings (behaviour).*

Let's put this overall ground rules formula in context.

1. Link them to organisational values

Most organisations have values, along with the strategic drivers of the business. They are the building blocks of a culture to be proud of. Although your team may have its unique opportunities, challenges, and characters, we are always part of a bigger picture, a bigger context, or as we say in "The Organisation Workshop," a bigger pond.

I strongly suggest the starting point of your own team ground rules is your own organisational values. List them down. There's normally three to seven. For each one, have a key behavioural (more on this later) ground rule, pertinent, exciting, and relevant to your team.

By doing that, you're letting your team know, "Hey, we are different from the other teams, and yet we are linked like other teams to the mother ship by a common set of values."

2. Start with where you are at

If your team has been working with each other for a while, there will be issues. In our team-focused leadership development programme "Our Best," I use the "Play of Life" technique, a brilliant creation of Dr Carlos Raimundo, which he outlines in *Relationship Capital* using dolls to tell the story of where the team is at.

You can also do this by surveys if you are little more left brain, or you can get the team together and ask them questions as a team.

1. What's working well?
2. What's not working so well?
3. What are your key frustrations with the team?
4. What have we got to do less of, do more of, or let go of altogether in order to get to the next level?

Start with where the team is at and make ground rules that address the surfaced issues. Do this by capturing all the issues on flip charts (yes, it's old technology, but the whole team needs to be looking up to a shared document, not looking down to an individual typed or electronic copy).

3. *Make them behaviourally specific*

If you're not careful, ground rules can be "word soup"—lots of broth but no real substance. It's great to come up with values such as honesty, service, pride, care, and integrity. But what do they really mean? Well, they mean different things to different people. That's why wherever possible, express your ground rules as specific behaviours—the more specific the better. I love the expression "You have to be able to put it in a wheelbarrow." What would I actually see you doing if I sat in on one of your one on ones or your team meetings?

Rather than simply saying, "We take pride in our achievements," with the value being pride, you could add a specific behaviour: "We take pride in our achievements by recognising individual and team performance at the earliest time we can."

"We consistently foster integrity in all that we do." With integrity as the value, it becomes: "We consistently foster integrity by going directly to a person we have a problem with, rather than talking to someone else."

Notice how we can "see" these behaviours. They are real.

Additionally, as the team matures (develops even stronger bonds of mutual trust and respect), the behaviours can change to suit the current context, with the values remaining the same.

4. Bring them to life

One way you can bring your team ground rules to life is through adverbs and verbs.

Yes, I know what you're thinking. Go back to school with me for a bit "Girls and boys, a verb is a doing word, and an adverb brings the doing word to life."

So you can go...

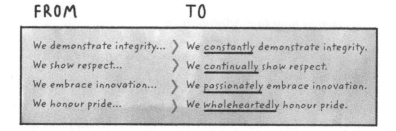

FROM	TO
We demonstrate integrity...	We <u>constantly</u> demonstrate integrity.
We show respect...	We <u>continually</u> show respect.
We embrace innovation...	We <u>passionately</u> embrace innovation.
We honour pride...	We <u>wholeheartedly</u> honour pride.

By using adverbs like constantly, continually, passionately, and wholeheartedly, you help to truly bring your ground rules to life. Simply having the dialogue about what verb and adverbs to add will help you clarify what you want to stand for as a team.

5. Make them real

It's essential your ground rules are in everyday language. I'd prefer colloquial expressions to those that are so formal it's like a straitjacket. And believe me, I've seen them, such as "We should discharge energy, if faced with an adverse situation, by engaging in dialogue with the other party involved."

What? What about "If we have a problem with someone, we tell them."

Only last week, I was looking at the website of a children's charity in Australia called Reach. One of their values struck me as very real. It wasn't about the amount they cared, the degree of compassion, or the community they intend to build. It simply read, "We give a shit."

It doesn't get much simpler than that. Do a reality check on your own ground rules.

6. Agree how to reinforce them

There's an old maxim in psychology: "What gets recognised gets repeated."

Yep, it's great. You've got this far and now have your five to nine behavioural ground rules in place. Complete them with verbs and adverbs to make them come to life, linked to organisational values and behaviourally specific.

So now what? How do you keep them alive? How do you make sure it was not just a futile exercise?

How do we keep them top of mind?

There are so many ways you can do this. What's vital is that the team owns them. To get this to happen, it's essential they come up with specific ways you'll keep them alive in your team.

Over the years, I've seen some fantastic ways of doing this, including but not limited to:

- Create an image of your ground rules and set it as your phone wallpaper
- Printing them on a wallet or purse card
- Laminating them and putting them on the wall
- Reviewing them at the beginning and end of a meeting
- Crediting those that are "walking breathing" role models of the ground rules
- Taking one ground rule at a time and talking about it at a team meeting
- Asking how certain team actions reinforce the values
- Reviewing everyone's performance that week or month against the values and behaviours
- Using them as a way to induct new team members

The list goes on and on, limited only by your team's imagination.

The trick is to bring the ground rules to life so that they become a meaningful yardstick to constantly answer the question: "How are we doing?"

7. Agree how to enforce them

A rule, any rule, is only as strong as the strength of conviction after it's broken. The 2016 Australian of the Year, Army Officer David Morrison, admitted he had "appropriated" the following line from Commander of the Defence Force and former NSW Governor David Hurley: "The standard you walk by is the standard you accept."

Well, it's exactly the same with your team ground rules. The ground rule that's broken, that you walk by, sets the standard you accept. You and your team set them in the first place.

I was out for dinner one night, talking Rugby Union with the Irish wife of a client. At one time, she worked for the BBC. She told me how she had been impacted by a line from Sir Clive Woodward, known for his meticulous attention to detail and for being the winning coach of the Rugby World Cup in 2003. He reported how one of the team ground rules in preparing for the 2003 World Cup was to "be on time" for training. When one player turned up late, he called with passionate intensity, "You just lost us the World Cup."

Now, you may think this is over the top, but surely the essence of it is not. The team came up with the ground rules, and they all agreed that the ground rules were what was going to help to get them to their goal. So why not be that strong? Why not enforce it? If not, what's the point of the ground rule in the first place? It's about being impeccable with your word.

I love the book *The Four Agreements* by Don Miguel Ruiz. One of the agreements is "Be impeccable with your word."

When your team agrees to ground rules, they are speaking their truth, and they are making agreements with each other. It's your integrity that's at stake. You've already encouraged the team to say exactly what they mean, to put the bowling balls on the table and then create ground rules to address those issues.

When a team member breaks a ground rule, whether consciously or unconsciously, you have to call it. If not, you and the whole team are not in integrity.

Earlier in my career, I worked with Price Waterhouse

Urwick, then the consulting arm of the international accounting firm Price Waterhouse (PW). I became very involved with "the differences that make the difference" in professional service firms like PW. What makes service firms successful?

That led me to the work of a David Maister. I read his books *Managing the Professional Services Firm* and *First Among Equals*. The one thing of all the information he shared in his books and seminars was, "Great businesses build cultures of intolerance."

With all our emphasis on people and the importance of empathy, you'd think it would read the other way round: "Great businesses build cultures of tolerance."

But let's take this a little further. Where do you draw the line?

This is where my baby boomer values seem to resurface. I can't believe how tolerant and complacent we have become in business and in life in general.

- Targets not hit: "the market's tough"
- Always late for work: "the buses keep breaking down"
- Shouting at colleagues: "that's just their style"
- Not cooperating with colleagues: "they've got so much on their plate"

The question for all of us is, "What are you tolerating in your team?"

Again, I draw on the work of Dr Ichak Adizes. Dr Adizes constantly refers to two aspects of management: decision making and implementation. His experience and research show that the best businesses and leaders have two different approaches to each of these key factors.

With decision making, it's important to involve as many representatives of key stakeholders as possible. In setting ground rules with your team, you must involve the whole team; you need to thrash them out together. It's a democracy, and that's part of the cathartic process. But once they're signed off on, you need to agree on what you are going to do if the rules are broken. How do you ruthlessly ensure implementation with dictatorial authority?

By the way, Dr Adizes puts these two styles together— democracy in decision making and dictatorship in implementation—and coined the portmanteau democraship.

I've seen a multitude of examples here, from yellow cards (first offence) and red cards (second offence) to monetary fines in a visible jar. For me, by far the best way to enforce, to hold people to the mast, is to agree on a process upfront.

For example, your steps could be:

1. Anyone can call you on your breaking a rule in private or in public in a team meeting.
2. You discuss it and leave it, or you discuss it and bring it to the team for further discussion.
3. If there is agreement that a rule was broken, you move on.
4. If not, after honest transparent discussion, it's "captain's call"—the team leader makes a decision either way.
5. The ground rule is both reinforced and enforced.

ENFORCING

And what if team members continually break the rules? Well, you go through the usual courtesy of seeking first to understand, but after several enforcements, it goes from a team issue to an individual performance issue, where your normal organisational policies would come into play. Avoid this like the plague. Really, it's an absolute last resort. Believe me: once it escalates to this level, it's hard coming back from here.

TIME FOR REFLECTION

Are you a stickler for rules? Are you Attila the Hun? Are you far too flexible, too tolerant? Are you too laid-back, too laissez-faire? Leadership really is a juggling act between flexibility and control. These are important questions to reflect on because your behaviour around rules will dramatically impact your success as a leader and your happiness as a human being. Again, it often goes back to your family of origin.

Rules have their place. Without them, the world would be in chaos.

Obviously, my mum and dad thought that when raising their two boys. My parents were both involved with World War II, with Dad on the Kokoda Trail and Mum a war nurse back in Australia. They were used to rules, to regulations, and they were used to obeying them. They thought it was their duty.

Therefore, it's not surprising we had rules in our household. There were only three. Did my brother and I abide by them? Not always. Did we agree with them? Not always. Were they clear? Absolutely. Were they reinforced? Every time we went out. Were they enforced? Yep. We were grounded numerous times, and Dad even threatened a belting. I can't remember that ever happening.

The rules were as follows.

1. Tell the truth.
2. Do as you're told.
3. Don't touch things that don't belong to you.

With rules, we have a hope of building and maintaining a civilised society where people can get on with their lives with reasonable certainty. Imagine if a country said, "You can drive on any side of the road you want to." Or imagine you're an Australian visiting the United States, and you still insist on driving on the left side of the road. This is not a very smart strategy. You'll crash into more than just cognitive dissonance if you keep that up!

Rules need to be made, but they need to be made around your context. Telling a millennial that one of the rules of the team is to "do as you're told" simply won't cut it. But here's the rub. The opposite may also be true for your personal and organisational success. I love the title of Marcus Buckingham's book *First Break All the Rules*. It's a provocation to remind us if we are too rule-bound, we will never break out of our current achievement level or box. Some rules simply don't cut it sometimes, and it's this degree of agility that often leads to breakthrough performance.

"I love the way you think outside of the box?"

"What box?"

What's vitally important here is to not marry the rules and divorce the outcome. We need to continually check the intent behind the rules and see whether they are helping to achieve the job they set out to do in the first place. It's a bit like in Italy, where I'm convinced a stop sign means an invitation to possibly slow down. Perhaps the real meaning of life is in the nuances, the spaces in between the rules.

THIRD WEEK: SMALL TWEAK 3

Again, these are exactly the seven steps you've read about already.

1. Let your team know you wish to gain involvement and commitment to how you are going to be with each other; where possible, link to your organisational values.

2. Get all the issues on the table; openly discuss what's working in the team, what's not and how it could be better. Start where you are at.

3. Make your ground rules behaviour specific to considerably increase understanding and adherence.

4. Bring the values to life by adding a descriptive word, an adverb to the agreed behaviour.
5. Don't get too fancy; make them everyday language, and make them real.
6. Agree how the team will keep them alive. How will you reinforce them?
7. Finally, what is the team code of behaviour when a ground rule is consciously or unconsciously broken? How will you reinforce them?

Now that

... you're totally present to everyone you are with;

... you're focussed to the point of being obsessed with, crediting great work and great qualities; and

...your team have agreed how you will work together;

it's time to focus your energy on creating stunning service and results for your clients and customers.

FACET 4: LEADING CLIENTS
DEMONSTRATE HEARTFELT CARING

You've all seen it. Put profit at the heart of your business, and you really won't be in business for that long. Put clients at the core and demonstrate heartfelt caring, and you're assured a brilliant reputation and, along with the appropriate systems, a brilliant business.

> *"You will get all you want in life if you help enough other people get what they want."*
> Zig Ziglar

But what do clients really want?

Well, they all want very different things, and they all want the same things. You see, although customers have unique, personalised needs, we've found those needs fit into a few specific categories and a logical hierarchy. Yes, it's a bit like our old favourite Maslow's Hierarchy of Needs in every psychology text and leadership programme. Over the years, I've taken our own experience and that of others to produce my very own Client Hierarchy of Needs. The key here is to exceed clients' expectations at every level of the hierarchy.

It's imperative that each need is satisfied without moving on to the next. In fact, trying to fulfil the next need up the hierarchy before fulfilling the one below often leads to mistrust, annoyance, and other disasters.

For each level, clients will have different reactions because of the different level of service you are providing and a judgement of that service. The pattern goes like this.

WHO IS YOUR CLIENT?

Great question. First, at *the human enterprise* we see clients differently. We don't see them as the corporation. We see them as the individual people within the organisation. They're not ABC Ltd or XYZ Ltd—they're Tom, Dick, and Harriet. They're individuals with individual tastes, desires, and needs.

Second, they're not just people who buy from you, be it tangible goods or services. They are anyone to whom you provide a service. Obviously I'd encourage you to apply this model to both internal and external clients. External clients are anyone outside the organisation to whom you provide a product or service, and internal clients are anyone within the organisation to whom you provide a product or service.

Your clients have four client needs that must be fulfilled to demonstrate heartfelt caring. Each one must be fulfilled before progressing to the next. It's a bit like *The Amazing Race*: if you don't complete the work at each station, you can't progress.

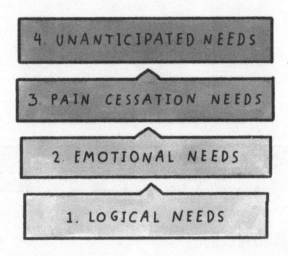

4. UNANTICIPATED NEEDS

3. PAIN CESSATION NEEDS

2. EMOTIONAL NEEDS

1. LOGICAL NEEDS

1. Logical needs

As the baseballers say, "This is the cost of getting into the ballpark." They are the minimum requirements (logical needs) that the client has of you. It's what they would expect to get from any provider. In fact, these needs don't really differentiate you, but their absence will have you being dropped in an instant. In this regard, they are like Herzberg's "satisfiers"—they don't really motivate, inspire, or engage you, but the absence of them will demotivate, disengage, and leave you uninspired.

Here are some examples of logical needs fulfilled that will have a different value for both your internal and external clients.

- You deliver fast and on time.
- You have a large selection.
- You deliver effective solutions.
- Your service is predictable.
- Your products or services are high quality.
- It's easy to get the information clients need.

2. Emotional needs

These are just that. Fulfilling these needs show you care about someone as a person, not just as a client with whom you're doing business. And it's well beyond the birthday e-mail. First, it could be remembering clients' name or knowing about their families. It could be asking about their hobbies outside of work—and not just because a superior told you to build rapport, but out of genuine interest. Here's a list of some emotional needs fulfilled.

- You do little things that say you care about me.
- I feel special dealing with you.
- You understand me when I'm in a hurry.
- You give me a sense of control.
- You listen to my situation or needs.
- I can deal with people, not machines.

As previously mentioned, at the time of updating this second edition we are in the height of the COVID-19 Pandemic. Although it's tough for everyone, it's a great opportunity to show how much you really care about your clients. Because

I can assure you, people will remember your kindness, your respect, your pragmatic optimism, long after the world goes back to a sense of normalcy. What will you do to show you truly care? How can you and your organisation better meet the emotional needs of your clients?

3. Pain cessation needs

There's an old maxim in business that we buy either to gain pleasure or to avoid or cease pain. Just as important as giving your customers what they want is also taking away the pain they are experiencing.

How do you do this? How do you know this? Well, you simply ask the following question: "What are the key frustrations you have doing business with someone like us?" This is a brilliant question, and I'll tell you why.

First of all, it assumes your customer has frustrations. That's always a good start, rather than thinking everything is hunky-dory. The mere asking of the question is a beautiful presupposition. It presupposes a frustration, and the client will begin to search for one—rather than simply asking, "Do you have any frustrations?" where the client has to answer yes or no, and often it's easier to take the no route.

Second, it presupposes that your customers could have several frustrations, not just one. As soon as they get the question, they are forced to think, "Let's see. I do have several frustrations. Which one shall I pick to discuss?"

Some of the biggest brand builders on the planet use this technique. Take the legendary story of Tom Monaghan, founder and ex-president of Domino's Pizza. (Yes, I know it's an oldie, but it's a goodie.) If you're under thirty, you may believe that we've always had hot, home-delivered pizza since the Stone Age. Not so.

You come home, and you don't want to cook. You think about ordering pizza. But then you think again because you're hungry enough to eat the whole pizza. You don't want to wait for almost an hour and then get cold pizza anyway. That's where Monaghan from Dominos Pizza came in. He recognised these key frustrations and did something about it. He improved his processes: the way pizza got into the oven, a huge local store network, and other new business practices, even down to using corrugated pizza delivery boxes to both protect the pizza and keep them warm.

> *"Delivering pizza fast is not a matter of driving fast,*
> *it's a matter of getting them in the oven fast."*
> Tom Monaghan

And that's where that early Dominos promise was born: hot pizza delivered to your door in thirty minutes or your money back. Notice that this has nothing to do with the quality of the pizzas and everything to do with alleviating the key frustrations of the customer.

4. Unanticipated needs

But perhaps the most powerful way to exceed clients' needs and demonstrate heartfelt caring is to show that you're thinking about them and what they need—long before they even realise it, and long before they have expressed it or asked for it. In doing so, you're creating what Seth Godin, author of *Purple Cow*, calls a remarkable business, one that people remark on to others.

It's so simple. More than any other gesture, it shows you really, truly care. It's when a client shares how his son is struggling at school, and you send him a contact who motivates kids to feel differently about themselves and teaches learning strategies. Or a client opens up about how she is struggling with her boss, and you send her an article on managing upwards or do some free coaching with her. Whatever the case, it has to be something you do for clients, not just talk about. As Scott Peck says in *The Road Less Travelled: A New Psychology of Love, Traditional Values and Spiritual Growth*, love is a doing word.

Here's another example. I arrive at a hotel, coughing a little. The doorman took the bags to the room and checked that we were all settled. Then around ten minutes later, there was a knock on the door.

"Who is it?" I asked.

"It's the porter, sir."

"Is everything all right?"

"Absolutely, sir. I just have a small gift for you."

I opened the door, and he handed me a pack of lozenges. "Mr Mitchell, I heard you coughing and could see it was uncomfortable, so I thought these may at least soothe your throat a little."

Now, the fact that he said all of this and didn't just hand me the lozenges is vital. We will look at that in a minute. I was blown away because it was totally unexpected. I offered him a tip, and he declined, saying, "Maybe next time, sir."

Let's look at why this is so powerful and the energy it creates. I once had a chat with one of the co-founders of

Shirlaws, an extremely successful global consulting firm. We were talking about meeting client needs, and we both agreed that giving something unexpected to a client says so much. It raises the energy and feelings of heartfelt caring to new levels. The co-founder then drew up a grid similar to the one pictured. With acknowledgement to Shirlaws, I'll share it here.

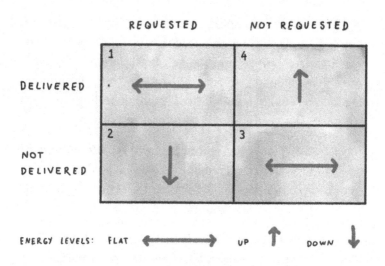

It's your standard four-box consulting model, yet it says so much. On the horizontal axis, you have whether or not a need was requested, and on the vertical axis you have whether or not you delivered that service. Within each of the four boxes, there is a certain energy created.

Box 1—If requested and delivered. Big deal. The energy is static.

Box 2—If requested and not delivered. Pissed off. The energy is down.

Box 3—Not requested, not delivered. Dah. It's a zero-sum game; the energy is again static.

Box 4—Not requested but delivered. Wow! You guys are remarkable.

The only way to get an uplift in energy, and therefore perception of service levels, is to deliver the unexpected.

There are whole books on customer service that can tell you how to do this, but as a leader, your role is pretty simple. Have your antennae out (we call it "situational sensing" in the "Why Should Anyone Be Led by You?" programme). Deliberately have an intention of listening, feeling, and seeing for unspoken needs. Then—and this is important:

1. **Don't say what you're going to do.** It's the surprise factor, or the fact that it's unanticipated, that makes it so remarkable. Remember that I had no idea that the porter was going to give me lozenges.

2. **Make the invisible visible.** Don't simply give the service and expect the client to link it back to you. When the thinking or thought behind the gesture is described, it makes the gesture even more powerful. Remember the porter didn't just say, "No worries." He made the invisible visible by describing the need he saw and then offering the solution to my pain.

After I've worked with clients for a while, I love doing those extra things for them. But not until those logical, emotional, and key frustration needs have been met.

COMBINING ALL FOUR CLIENT NEEDS

Many great businesses have been built on meeting their clients' logical, emotional, pain cessation, (their key frustrations), and unanticipated needs. Ever taken your damaged car to a panel beater? Your logical need is to have your car fixed. Your emotional need is to be treated as an individual and to have your personal situation considered. Your key frustration is not having a car to drive while yours is being repaired. The clever repairers will give you a replacement vehicle until yours is ready. Pain cessation need met! But what are the unanticipated needs?

Years ago, I took my damaged car to a panel beater on Sydney's North Shore, and I experienced all four client needs being met in the most unusual way. The first three needs were met as above, but here's where it got interesting. You see, the owner was into old classic cars. Over the years, he had collected them all: Morris Minors, Triumph Heralds, Fiat Bambinos, Wolseleys, Buicks, Dodges, Old Fords, Mark 2 and Mark 5 Jaguars, and even an old XK 120 Jaguar. All were in working order. The best thing was that I got to choose my replacement vehicle. Wow! Unanticipated needs met!

And what do you think I remarked on? The logical quality of the panel beating and spray painting? No way! It was the retro car I drove for a week. Because in that one week, I was young again, transported back to those times of heightened emotion and a simpler way of being. All this from a panel beating business. Here's what this looks like visually in what I call Mitchell's Client Needs Hierarchy™.

MITCHELL'S CLIENT NEEDS HIERARCHY

CLIENT NEEDS	CLIENT REACTION	JUDGEMENT OF YOUR SERVICE LEVEL
UNANTICIPATED NEEDS	AMAZEMENT	REMARKABLE
PAIN CESSATION NEEDS	RELIEF	AWESOME
EMOTIONAL NEEDS	DELIGHT	GREAT
LOGICAL NEEDS	SATISFACTION	GOOD

In the first column, you have the hierarchy of client needs. To the right is the feelings your clients experience as a result of meeting those needs, and in the last column is how they judge your service levels and the words they would use to describe it to others.

I truly believe no matter what leadership role you're in, whether it be research and development, supply chain, marketing, finance, HR, or sales, we all have customers or clients. Meeting their needs should be at the heart of everything you do as a leader. But it's only when you exceed client needs that you fully demonstrate your heartfelt caring.

TIME FOR REFLECTION

I've talked so much about looking after clients that I'm going to look like I'm going troppo on you and say exactly the opposite now. It's taken me a long while to realise it, but some clients simply aren't worth looking after.

I'm not being defeatist, but after having spent over thirty-five years trying to please clients and being a bit of a pleaser in general, I've finally realised you can't please everybody.

"I can't give you a recipe for success, but I can give you one for failure—try to please everybody."
Herbert Bayard Swope

We've all had clients—and I've certainly had my share—who were very demanding, who didn't return phone calls, who got stuff to you at the last moment, or who asked for a set fee and then placed further expectations on you beyond the original brief.

Then the payment cycle got longer and longer: two weeks, a month, three months. At times, we've had to chase overdue billings for six months, and that was from major corporations.

I saw these clients as a challenge, I'd win them over, and I'd try even harder. It rarely worked. It drained me and our team. All the time, my other clients who truly wanted to work in a partnering manner got less and less attention. Yet they paid on time, they took me into their trust, they returned phone calls, they referred others to *the human enterprise*, they gladly gave us testimonials, and they sometimes even entertained us.

Why is it that the people (including friends and family) who matter most are right under our noses, and we just don't see it? Why do we give them so little attention just because they don't often demand it? Like a spouse you've known for years, you begin to take for it granted. Don't do it.

Nurture them and show them heartfelt caring. A good way to do this is to fire the clients who don't work for you. Now, don't get so arrogant that you go up and say, "You're fired," like in *The Apprentice*. But unless you are desperate, don't work with them anymore; let them slip away. Put your energy into the clients who are a joy to work with and where there is a true spirit of partnership. Choose clients who will call you first even though you may not be the right provider.

Why? Because you can't continue to provide heartfelt service to those you perceive as heartless clients. Believe me, you'll eventually get resentful, which is really just emotion coming back on yourself. Then you'll get demotivated, tired, depressed, and even sick. You can't give heartfelt service in a depressed or sick state. Neither can your people or your team.

I love it when leaders support their teams in not putting up with disrespectful or rude clients and customers. Sure, sometimes things go wrong, and it's important to allow people to let off steam—but not for too long, and not at you or your team. It's impossible to totally respect yourself if you are constantly being disrespected by others. Sure, work it out, talk it through, and remain in partnership. But if you've done all you can do, walk away. Life is too short.

I've been teaching, coaching, and facilitating for a long while now. I still love it, and I absolutely love my clients. I've also fired a few along the way, along with people in our own business. I know I would never have been in the game and still be as passionate if I'd let certain clients get the better of me. If your clients are internal, it's tough; you can't simply walk away. But you can tell them exactly how you feel and talk about how they will get great service if you work together. Note that service doesn't mean servile.

You particularly have to manage expectations upfront, or else you're going to have some really long days. I know it may feel difficult when you're starting out in your business or when you're in a new role. But if you can truly work together right from the start and be in partnership, then your energy, your longevity, your reputation, and your joy will continue to spark year after year. That's the place from where all heartfelt service comes.

FOURTH WEEK: SMALL TWEAK 4

1. List all your key clients or customers down the left side of the page. We want personal names—Tom, Dick, and Harriet—not customers' names like Woolworths, Salesforce, Red Bull, and L'Oreal.
2. Across the top of the page horizontally, write the four key needs: logical, emotional, key frustrations and unanticipated.
3. By yourself, or even better with your team, fill in the table.
4. Once completed, list all the potential actions you could do to truly demonstrate heartfelt caring.
5. Then just do it!

See chart next page.

Now you're fully present, and you're crediting your associates, you've got your team ground rules in place, and you're demonstrating heartfelt caring to customers, it's time to look at how to lead the whole organisation.

Client Names	ACTIONS FOR CLIENT CARE				
	Logical Needs	Emotional Needs	Pain Cessation Needs	Unanticipated Needs	
1.					
2.					
3.					
4.					

FACET 5: LEADING THE ORGANISATION
FOSTER COLLABORATION ACROSS BOUNDARIES

People often say, "Never look back." I don't agree. I think it's incredible to look back and see how much you've developed as a person, as a leader. Recognise the friendships you've cultivated, the ones you've let go of, and the lessons learnt.

One of my retrospectives is how much I thought I knew about business before I started my own. I didn't realise what a narrow frame of reference I viewed work through. Even though I had previously worked in the consulting group Price Waterhouse Urwick, which was predominantly an accounting practice, I knew very little about the numbers. No, I was the people person, the engagement evangelist, the HR hero, the culture champion.

That was great until about three months into my own business, in September 1987. My twenty-thousand-dollar overdraft I'd secured with the family home hit nineteen thousand, and the bank manager rang me. We had our daughter, Ruby, aged three years old, and Deborah was pregnant with our son, Abe. I had to make this work. I had too much to lose. He politely and respectfully informed me of the current overdrawn balance and said very firmly, "We will take your house, you know. You do realise that." Well, I guess I knew it on one level, but I really didn't think they would be that nasty. And of course, what it would mean for me was no home for our growing family. Perhaps that's negative motivation, but it worked. Now, I realise most people in the corporate world don't have their family homes on the line, but you do have your jobs and your financial security.

It was a huge wake-up call for me. After three months of playing entrepreneur, I quickly secured some work, got the overdraft down, and learnt about one of the most important facets of business. It's one that I truly believe every leader needs to master: cash flow.

Here was the problem: I wasn't thinking like a business leader. I was thinking like a technician, in this case a specialist in leadership development. This was my passion, and it still is. But let me assure you that one of the main reasons companies, from small businesses to major corporates, can get into trouble is because the leaders don't bother trying to make business people out of everyone, from receptionist to experienced directors. This is one of the missions of *Leaders for Life*.

A WHOLE NEW SET OF SKILLS

Michael Gerber's brilliant small business book, *The "E" Myth*, says people who set up their own business are technicians suffering from entrepreneurial seizures. Well, the same could be said for many managers. They are technicians (IT,

HR, supply chain, finance, customer development, legal, or marketing) suffering from "leadership seizures." Because they are great engineers, they and the organisation think they will make great leaders of other engineers. The truth is that it requires a whole different set of skills, or if not skills, a whole new way of looking at business. It's also why you can recognise a future leader very early in their career. They are focussed on solutions, not problems. They get that the 'content' of the issue in their functional area, is not half as important as the total organisational context in which it occurs. They always make the future bigger than their function.

But it's not just that technicians are placed in leadership roles without any leadership skills. No, it's bigger than that. It's because they are often unaware that they see the world primarily through their functional lenses. Abraham Maslow summed this up beautifully, and you've probably heard it before:

"I suppose it is tempting, if the only tool you have is a hammer, to treat everything as if it were a nail."

We constantly forget to step back and see how the context we are in impacts both our behaviour and our results.

I remember when I started my own business. Everything was a "people problem" because that was the lens through which I viewed the world. It was my training, my experience, and my identity; that was my hammer. Cash flow? Well, I didn't really know about it, and I didn't really care. That was for the accountants, the bean counters. But cash flow is a law of business, and as any lawyer will tell you, ignorance is no excuse for breaking the law. I had broken the law. And if you're still wondering what the law of cash flow is, it's very simple: "At one time in the life of the business, revenue collected must exceed costs incurred." The number of businesses that go bust because they break this rule, the number of share floats that go belly up, and the number of people who get truly burnt is incredible.

What's the solution? Again, it's amazingly simple and elegant. Get everyone in the business stepping into other people's shoes, seeing the world through multiple functional lenses. Increase their perspective-taking capability. Increase their ability to see context.

> *"If you can learn a simple trick, you'll get along a lot better with all kinds of folks. You never really understand a person until you consider things from his point of view— until you climb into his skin and walk around in it."*
> Atticus Finch in *To Kill a Mockingbird*

Although this chapter of the book is possibly the most business focused, it doesn't mean we've left the heart-centred leadership behind. Not at all. When you put your heart and soul into understanding someone else's point of view, someone else's perspective, it immediately says you care. People pick up on your intention and your willingness to see where they are coming from. Nothing builds trust and mutual respect more than genuinely being interested and asking about someone's worldview. Watch what your willingness to climb into their skin and walk around in it does for your relationships.

WHOLE SYSTEMS THINKING

One of the fastest ways I know of doing this is to get people to become whole systems thinkers. We continually emphasise this idea in all our leadership development programmes. I first came across this through the work of Marvin Weisbord in *Productive Workplaces: Organising and Managing for Dignity, Meaning, and Community*. It requires leaders to look at every major (and sometimes minor) business decision through other filters or lenses, rather than just their own.

Nothing builds commitment and collaboration across organisational boundaries like a leader who has respectfully assessed a problem or opportunity in terms of its impact or possible benefits to the whole system, because it forces the leader to take others' worlds into account. It's a bit like taking photos and putting different filters on your camera. It's the same picture, but every one of the filters gives you a different perspective. For example, with fly fishing, you can certainly work the stream without sunglasses. But put on a pair of polarised lenses, and it's almost a miracle. You can see beneath the surface of the water so much easier. You can see the fish. (For me, catching them is another issue.) You get to see the real business issue, what's beneath the surface. Or what about X-rays? They still blow me away. Fancy looking at a broken leg with just your eyes, knowing you were in pain, but then the X-ray gets beneath the surface and tells you exactly where the break is. Well, that's the impact of trying on different lenses.

So, what is whole systems thinking? It's knowing that everything is attached to everything else. Touch the system anywhere, and you impact it everywhere. Fixing something somewhere can often create a problem somewhere else in the system.

Let's take a real business example in the late 1980s. (For those of you who can't remember, we had incredibly high interest rates in Australia and a mini-recession in 1987, the year I started my business. Great timing!) I had a client cancel an annual conference due to financial constraints. They couldn't afford it. But the conference was part of the fabric of the place; it was in their DNA, and it was an annual ritual where results were reviewed, people's efforts were recognised, and people partied. With this client, they really partied.

If you just look at it through a financial lens and not a whole system lens, this was a tough but responsible decision. But here's what happened: the decision impacted morale, which was fading anyway. In turn, people dropped their standards and their attention to detail. This in turn affected customer satisfaction. Customers not only felt it, but they saw it in mistakes in documentation. This impacted reputation and the brand. Word of mouth is still a powerhouse in the marketplace. This meant fewer customers, and of course fewer customers meant less revenue and profit. The very problems they were trying to address in the first place were amplified even more by their decision to cut the conference.

> *"Nowadays, people know the price of everything*
> *and the value of nothing."*
> Oscar Wilde

I see this time and time again, when unenlightened large corporates or private equity firms take over smaller entrepreneurial businesses built on soul. They invariably look at the business through a cost-cutting lens, rarely considering that the real value of the business is its DNA and the relationships forged over many years of sweat equity.

Was it the wrong decision? Maybe, maybe not. The point is that had the decision been approached from a whole systems perspective, would it have been made? Could there have been another alternative? Could the potential fallout have been thought through, and could strategies have been put in place to counteract the fallout or potential implications?

A whole systems decision would have addressed all of these issues and more. So what are the lenses through which we should view both problems and possibilities?

There are four main lenses I'd suggest you use in your organisation and, more important, encourage everyone else to look through. They are both separate and interconnected. The first three come from Weisbord, and the fourth, from Peter Block.

1. Economic
2. Technical
3. Social
4. Political

Let's review them in enough detail to give you a feel for each one. Again, irrespective of where the issue shows up, you should apply these four filters. You will make much better business decisions, gain much more support, foster greater collaboration across what can sometimes be boundaries, increase your business wisdom, and considerably increase your reputation as a business and not just a functional leader.

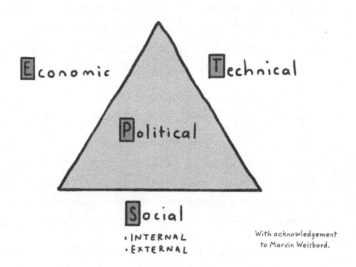

E conomic   T echnical

P olitical

S ocial
• INTERNAL
• EXTERNAL

With acknowledgement to Marvin Weisbord.

ECONOMIC

Every issue has economic implications for:

- Revenue
- Costs
- Margins
- Profitability
- Return on investment
- Cash flow
- Long-term equity (value of the business)

Put your accounting and finance glasses on and unleash the bean counter within. Yes, really. In fact, when mentoring new leadership development consultants or anyone in people and culture, one of my first pieces of advice is to learn to speak and read the two key languages of business.

1. The profit and loss statement
2. The balance sheet

Unless it is a private company (and even then, we have what is known as "open book management"), imagine the difference it would make to the decision-making of every member of the organisation if they thought about the short-term and long-term economic implications of their decisions.

If you're a leader, start "finance for non-finance manager" workshops in your organisation.

TECHNICAL

It's important to point out this is not just technology, although it involves technology. It's simultaneously thinking through your issue, challenge, idea, or decision and its impact on issues such as:

- Standards
- Processes
- Innovation
- Quality
- Efficiencies
- Documentation
- Intellectual property
- Information technology
- Plant and equipment

SOCIAL

This lens is obviously about the people and has two aspects to it: social internal, which is the internal people side of the organisation, and social external, the people outside the immediate organisation or team.

For social internal, we have such factors as:

- Morale
- Engagement
- Culture
- Excitement
- Talent strength
- Bench strength (succession)

Social external includes such factors and people as:

- Brand
- Reputation
- Social purpose
- Service levels
- Customers
- Consumers
- Governance
- Suppliers

POLITICAL

Many see political as a subset of social, yet over the years, I've begun to realise that organisations are so political that it's important enough to have this as a separate lens. I want to make a distinction here, as Peter Block does in *The Empowered Manager*—a brilliant read about positive versus negative politics.

Block tells us negative politics shows up in such ways as:

- Saying yes when you mean no
- Withholding information
- Speaking directly to higher authorities and not informing your boss
- Name dropping as manipulation
- Benefits without concessions
- Tough or tender face

According to Block, positive politics is "The advocacy of your function and the gaining of support for your personal and organisational goals." It involves four key stands.

1. Having your own vision of greatness.
2. Being real and authentic.
3. Being a living, breathing role model of the values you espouse.
4. Managing all your stakeholders differently based on trust and agreement.

It requires leaders making decisions or considering impacts and consequences to ask such questions as:

- Who's vulnerable?
- Who could get hurt?
- Whose power may be impacted?
- Who do we need to get on side?
- Who has the itch, the pain that needs to be scratched?
- Where is the energy?
- Who has the ear of the final decision-maker?
- Who will have final authority?
- Who will make it happen and be responsible for implementation?
- Whom do we need to check in with, or at least consult?
- Whom do we need to at least inform?

Two of the biggest objections that come up again and again when people meet resistance to their ideas is "Why wasn't I asked?" and "Why wasn't I told?".

By now you've no doubt picked up my love of mnemonics to make life as simple, practical, and memorable as possible. Here's another one based on the idea that whole systems thinkers really get to the heart of the issue. They don't take yes (or no, for that matter) for an answer. They look beyond the immediate issue and think about decisions and actions from a much larger perspective.

You'll sometimes be seen as a bit annoying, sometimes frustrating to deal with, a disruptive thinker, an irritant, or a pest. Good! Great! That's your job. Your role is to be a systems PEST, which stands for:

Political
Economic
Social
Technical

Ironically enough, the more of a PEST you are, the more you'll help to foster collaboration across boundaries. Lately, I've seen many leaders add another two lenses: environmental and legal. So, I guess it becomes PESTEL.

TIME FOR REFLECTION

One of the things we most cling to in life is our identity. We find it too silly or uncomfortable at a party to ask, "Who are you?" and we probably couldn't answer that question anyway. Therefore, we ask, "What are you?" Well, not as bluntly as that. Normally it's "What do you do for a living?".

Then we make quantum leaps in logic about the sort of person to whom we are talking. From there, we make up all sorts of characteristics about the person we have just met, based on our past stereotyping of the traits of those in those sorts of roles or occupations.

Your accountants are into money and finances, your engineers are into building or blowing up things, your HR people are into people of course, and those in advertising are our crazy creatives.

Why is this? Well, it's because although we have this huge need for change and being surprised, we also have this huge need for certainty and stability. It's not only for who others are but for who we are. Our need to hold onto our self-concept, our personal identity, is mind-blowing even though it may not serve us.

Years ago, I was introduced to the concept of recidivism in the gaol system. A social worker told me that even though prisoners may have a low self-esteem and feel unworthy, recidivists' self-concepts are in fact very strong. A recidivist is a convicted criminal who reoffends, especially repeatedly. They see themselves as an offender and recommit crimes to be put back in gaol. Because it's gaol that literally and figuratively houses their identity.

And you know what? I also see this in the corporate world, where leaders hang onto their identities. Irrespective of their seniority as leaders, they see themselves as salespeople, as engineers, or as marketers. They continue to see the world through this lens and the filters that go with it. An ex-General Manager of Sales becomes the new Managing Director and states very clearly, "You are either selling or serving someone who is selling." He doesn't even think about how this will land with those in supply chain. Most in supply chain, believe it or not, see it as repugnant and a real put-down.

Whole systems thinking is so much more than a way of viewing the world of business. It's a chance to totally transform your identity, which as I previously said is one of the hardest things to let go of—and one of the most liberating things when you do.

Imagine what it would be like to take on a whole new identity, that of a whole system thinker, the total business leader in every sense of the word. You do it so much so that after twelve months, you were almost unrecognisable to yourself.

FIFTH WEEK: SMALL TWEAK 5

Next time an important business decision needs to be made, consider the whole system and at the very least simply ask yourself (or those around you) five simple questions. Yes, you may unsettle a few feathers, but as a *Leader for Life*, that's part of your role as a real PEST.

1. Political: What, if any, are the political implications of this issue?
2. Economic: What, if any, are the economic implications of this issue?
3. Social: What, if any, are the internal people implications of this issue?
4. Social: What, if any, are the external people implications of this issue?
5. Technical: What, if any, are the technical implications of this issue?

You've now completed the small tweaks pertaining to organisational life. You're totally present, you're showing appreciation and giving credit, you've set ground rules for your team, you're really demonstrating heartfelt caring for customers as people just like you, and you're fostering collaboration across boundaries through whole systems thinking.

Now it's time to get personal.

FACET 6: LEADING FAMILY & FRIENDS
BE THEIR CHAMPION

There are very few people who could look you straight in the eye and tell you that life is all about work. My dear mentor, coach, and friend Dr Fred Grosse puts it this way: "Life is primary, business is secondary. Business funds life."

In the book *The Top Five Regrets of the Dying*, Bronnie Ware, a palliative care specialist who worked for many years with people in the last three to twelve weeks of their lives, shares some profound insights. Here are two of them.

1. All of the men nursed deeply regretted spending so much of their lives on the treadmill of a work existence.
2. Often, they did not realise the full benefit of old friends until their dying weeks, and it was not possible to track them down. Many had become so caught up in their own lives that they had let golden friendships slip by over the years. There were many deep regrets about not giving friendships the time and energy they deserved.

What about you? Has your work life become so busy, so frenetic, that you're not making enough time for friends and family? You will regret it.

> *"No other success can compensate for failure in the home."*
> David O. McKay

Surely one of our biggest goals in life should be to live a life of no regrets. Of all the facets of *Your Leadership Diamond*, this is the one that will ultimately give you the most joy and the most heartache if you gloss over it. If you're not vigilant, you'll experience the most pain and the most regrets unless you fail to polish it. The funny thing about polishing this facet is that it really doesn't take much effort at all. It's very simple: be their champion.

This will be different for each and every one of us, but basically, it's being their biggest supporter in any endeavour or in anything that's really important to them, not you.

FOUR WAYS TO BE THEIR CHAMPION

There are many ways of doing this. Here are four of my favourites.

1. Show up.
2. Help their kids.
3. Be their greatest supporter.
4. Be there in times of need.

1. *Show Up*

You've heard the saying that 80 per cent of success is showing up. Well, let me put it another way: 80 per cent of having great families and friends is showing up. Show up for your partner, your kids, your friends, and your extended family.

In coaching senior executives, there's a stand I take more strongly than any other, and that's insisting that leaders be there for their family and friends, that they lead in all areas of their lives. The leaders (typically men) tend to make all sorts of excuses: "It's a difficult period at work right now." "After the restructure is completed." "It's quarter end and not a good time." "We are down two key team members at present." I've heard them all. But I've also heard about divorces and separations and the pain, particularly if kids are involved.

There are special moments in life that you will never get back. If you're a parent, it's the school play where your kid played the part of the lead tree, their first netball game, dropping them off for their first day of school, dropping them off at their year twelve graduation. These are the moments you'll remember on your death bed. These are precious gems that all the money in the world won't buy.

I'll let you in on a secret: your kids (or your sibling's kids, or your friend's kids) won't remember the size of the house you lived in, the car you drove, or the brand of wine you drank. What they will remember is the time you spent with them. The holidays, throwing around a ball in the backyard, the dress-ups, the sleepovers at your place, you doing canteen duty, you yelling from the sidelines at every match, you clapping loudest at every performance. You showing up.

Please don't miss these magical moments.

I've received a few awards along the way in life, but one of the ones I'm proudest of is my "Greatest Supporter" award from my son's school when he was playing hockey. Now, I wasn't one of those ugly parents yelling obscenities from the sidelines, but if you know me, I can be a little over the top at times. My son's team made it into the grand final—an achievement in its own right. Few of us get to play in grand finals in our lives. To me, this was an international showdown. Your key role as a parent is to embarrass your kids. That's something I've gotten really good at. On that day, I'm convinced that me waving the Australian flag and singing "Waltzing Matilda" is what led them all to that grand final victory.

It probably was a bit too full on, but you get the idea. Show up, and when you do, show up fully. At the beginning of the year, put the holidays in the diary, find out when parent-teacher nights are, and schedule to be there for those sporting and key school events. See these times as the most important appointments in your diary, because they are.

2. Help their kids

This obviously doesn't apply to all of us. You may not have kids, and neither may your friends. But I've always felt one of the greatest ways of saying thanks and showing appreciation is to help friends' children.

I love our friends' kids; they really are like our own. There's something marvellous when thirty-plus-year-olds still call us Uncle Mitch and Aunty Deb. They still remember the silly magic tricks we did with them as kids, the coins we pulled out of their ears, or the ridiculous costumes we wore to their parties.

At the time, we were just having fun and making our kids feel loved and appreciated. It was only years later that I appreciated how precious these moments were and the beautiful memories they were creating.

If you really want to show great leadership and great love to your friends, help their kids. You have no idea what it will mean to them. And as selfish as it is, you'll get such a buzz out of it. You see, sometimes kids need more than just their parents to show them the way. It really does take a whole village to raise a child.

Stephen Biddulph, in *Raising Boys,* tells us how young men need the company of older men such as uncles or friends to reinforce values their own fathers may have passed on. They should be there as positive role models. Sometimes they should simply be available to talk with when the relationship with the kids' own mum and dad may have broken down. Support them and barrack for them in their hobbies, sporting, and professional endeavours. Show them just how much you care about their parents and the honour and privilege of having lifetime friends.

Perhaps in their later years, it could be making introductions for them, helping them network, and primarily taking an interest in them and what they are up to. My old mates really are like old blankets: we're all a little worn around the edges, but we wouldn't swap out warmth for quids. And every time we catch up, it's the usual "How are you?" Then we talk about the kids, always with an ear to how we can help.

3. Be their greatest supporter

As much as you love your family and friends, let's face it: some of them are into really weird stuff. But remember that it's not weird to them; they love it. One of the greatest leadership acts you can ever do is to support your friends and family in the pursuit of their dreams. Show an interest in their careers, hobbies, interests, and sports. By celebrating their achievements, you celebrate them. Deborah, my wife, told me this great saying when I first met her about forty years ago: "If you're going to go through life, celebrate. And if you're going to celebrate, celebrate the opening of an envelope."

What demonstrates great leadership is your encouragement and your sharing in their excitement, their passion. We love to celebrate birthdays with our nearest and dearest. Our friends all make a fuss about each other. We genuinely care about their wins, their trials and tribulations. Most of all, we listen and barrack passionately for them from the sidelines.

4. *Be there in times of need*

There is no greater feeling of comfort than friends showing up in times of need. We will all have these times in our lives: an illness in the family, a job loss, a business crisis, a relationship break-up, a divorce, or feeling a bit lost in the world. Be there in times of need. Most times, you don't have to even talk; simply being there is enough. Wherever possible, I try to be there for family and friends at these times.

Deborah, Abe (our son), and I will be forever grateful for when people just showed up after we lost our daughter, Ruby, following neurosurgery. Sometimes they would sit with us—no words or advice, just lots of tears, hugs, and cups of tea. "Hey, thinking of you. Won't stay for long. Cooked you a lasagne for dinner."

Maybe you're like me, and at times you get caught up in chasing bright, shiny objects—the new suit, new car, new boat, or new house. There's nothing's wrong with ambition. But if you're chasing these objects to fill your empty soul, it will never be full. We both know that at the end of the day, these objects really do amount to nothing. We come into this world with nothing, and we leave with the same.

The real riches of our lives will be time spent with family and friends and the relationships we nurture. Can you ever put a price on such friendships? The regret of not showing up in times of need will linger well past the temporary relief of attending to the myriad of never-ending business issues whose pull seems so overpowering at the time.

TIME FOR REFLECTION

There's a mate of mine who calls me out of the blue from his VW (he's been driving VWs all his adult life) on his way home from work. He calls for no reason; it's simply to just see how I am, how the family is, and what am I up to. He's a real mate. As a business owner, he's just as busy as the rest of us. But he makes the time.

He's the sort of person you go to when you want advice, or counsel when you want the truth. He's always the first to support me in my or my family's efforts. I want to be like that, and so should you.

This is a generalisation, but I see a lot of people in the corporate world not developing their friendships outside of that world. They don't make the calls to friends, and they don't make the time. When they retire, they struggle with the realisation that people don't call them anymore. They were only ever called for what they were, their role, not who they were.

Their currency drops immediately when they no longer have CEO on their business card.

I've got a lot of mates, and I care for them dearly, but I've become clearer and clearer on the sort of friends with whom I want to spend my time.

Someone who helped me gain clarity on this was Dr Carlos Raimundo, who wrote the book *Relationship Capital*. I remember in one of his workshops, he put up a four-box matrix. I won't draw it up; we're supposed to be reflecting here. On one axis was the amount of fun, pleasure, and joy you got being around people, from low to high. On the other axis was how much the person stretched you, motivated you, and challenged you to grow, again from low to high.

Now, this is going to sound very callous, and even shallow, but you can't afford to have too many friends in the wrong boxes. I'm not saying you should totally cut people out of your life, but you have to minimise your contact with negative nellies. This allows you to spend time with the friends (and even family) who are good for your self-esteem, energy, and soul.

The friends who suck up your energy and don't stretch you? Enough said. Friends that don't give you much joy but are always challenging you? Yeah, they're important, but you can only take so much. And the fun ones with no stretch? Great for parties, but they probably don't take you to greater heights, to a better place.

Of course, that leaves friends who challenge you to be your best, support you and your family, and have a generosity of spirit that makes them a joy to be around. They are the jewels, and they are the precious ones. Let them know it any way you can.

"Show me your friends and I'll show you your future."

We seem to be developing a world that loves quantity over quality. Having thousands of Facebook friends, more likely acquaintances, may make you think you're popular, but it will never give you the joy that a few precious mates will.

It's like business owners who think they're doing well because their website has had so many hits. Yet those who get the importance of quality know that HITS stand for How Idiots Track Success.

As my wife and soul mate for over forty years says, you have to find your tribe. Find the place where you can truly be accepted for who you are: in the bosom of pals and possibilities.

"You become like the people you spend the most time with."
Jack Canfield

Sorry to be so harsh, but you also may need to stop being such an "idiot" about who your friends are. Hang with those who both give lovingly of themselves and receive you lovingly for who you are.

SIXTH WEEK: SMALL TWEAK 6

Now that you've got your business life sorted, wasn't it great to think about your home life? Perhaps we should have started here.

With this tweak, I want you to take out your diary. I want you to make sacrosanct annual family holidays, weekend retreats, birthdays, anniversaries—you name it.

Every week, once a week for the next three months, call a friend to chat and say hi. Listen to how you can best support them, how you can be there for them. Then just do it.

Now for polishing the final facet of *Your Leadership Diamond* ...

FACET 7: LEADING COMMUNITY
HONOUR YOUR CALLING

To me, this is where you really get what it means to leave a legacy well beyond work. Many leaders I meet convince themselves that they're too busy to do community work right now, but when it slows down a bit or when they retire, they're looking forward to the opportunity to contribute.

This sort of response always saddens me for a number of reasons. One, you don't get to make the incredible contribution to the world you could make with your skills right now. Our world needs you! Two, you probably believe things will slow down, stabilise, and get easier. My firm belief and experience is that this is an absolute fallacy. It never stops or slows down. And three, you deny yourself the joy, the elation, the sense of community that comes from nurturing your generosity of spirit.

The answer? Rather than continually putting it off till sometime in your imaginable future, do it now. That's why part of our passion at *the human enterprise* is to have every leader we touch give back to their community in some way.

But where do you start?

Well, start early. I firmly believe one of the greatest leadership lessons you can teach young graduates, in any discipline is to do charity work, right from the beginning of their careers. Particularly if they are aspiring, achievement-oriented, ambitious and in far too much of a hurry to get a car and the corner office. Firstly, it's good for the world, and secondly, and most importantly, you'll never be a great leader unless you learn to be a great follower. The best leaders are there for others, not themselves. They are the ultimate volunteers. In fact, that is leadership, full stop.

Leading in your community can take many forms. There are many communities you can be involved with. But before we look at a specific strategy on how to get you involved, let me give you a few hints that will make your contribution much more engaging and effective.

DONATIONS ALONE ARE NOT ENOUGH FOR LEADERS FOR LIFE

Sure, it's a great start. Charities want and need your dough. But chequebook charity is never enough. It's only the starting point for leaders. In many ways, simply writing out a cheque is a form of releasing the discomfort you may feel for not getting more directly involved.

Don't get me wrong, it's a great start. But if this is all you do, and if you do it begrudgingly (as I see some leaders do), then it will never leave you with the deep feelings of joy you can get from giving of your time, your energy, your passion, and yourself.

TOO MANY CHARITIES SPOIL THE BROTH

If you're like me, you'll have people writing to you or phoning you two to three times a week and asking for a donation. Here's the dilemma. Mostly they are very worthy causes, so how do you choose? Whom do you give to? Even if just giving money is not enough, you still have to choose when you do.

To make the most of your donations, I suggest you choose one to two charities to give to at any one time. And by time, I'm talking about a minimum of one to three years. That way when they phone you at home, you can graciously say, "Thank you for the opportunity. I really think it's great what you are doing. Yet we currently support our charity of choice, Starlight Children's Foundation." (Or whatever your focus is at that time.) I found that this:

1. Makes me feel less guilty for saying no.
2. Often has the caller saying, "Oh, that's great. Thanks for that." (And I assume it doesn't make them feel as rejected or put off by bad vibes.)
3. Helps you really get to know about what specific charities do, who the people are that are running it, and what the goals are. And of course, it makes it easier to get more involved in their fundraising activities. And important for all leaders, you get to know where the money goes. How is your donation put to good use? In fact, it's always a great question to ask, "What percentage of the actual revenue or money raised goes to the cause compared to the day-to-day overheads and expenses?" This is difficult to find out if you spread yourself too thinly.

So how do you choose how to be involved? I genuinely believe this is easy. Here are four questions to help you narrow your focus on how to get involved. I'll give you some examples of how I've applied these four questions over the years to various charities that may trigger some possibilities for you.

KEY QUESTIONS TO ASK

1. *The Cause: Your Passion*—what is a cause or worldly condition that I care deeply about?

2. *Skills and Knowledge*—what are some skills or knowledge I have that could be useful to this cause?

3. *Applications and Usage*—how could I apply my skills or knowledge to make a difference?

4. *The First Step*—what's the first step I can take to begin to make a contribution?

1. Choose your passion: the cause

Choosing a cause that has deep significance for you is the first vital step to making a contribution. This is the first step in leaving a legacy where you psychologically begin to move from success to significance, from making money to making meaning.

A great starting point is to begin with your own family or friends. Is there an illness or condition in your own family that has an aligned charity you can get involved with? My dad had Alzheimer's disease. He was a big, physical bloke who had survived the jungles of New Guinea in World War II on the Kokoda Trail, and to see him slowly deteriorate over the years broke all of our hearts. But Mum never stopped caring for him. It was what Mace and Rabins called *The 36-Hour Day*, the title of their book on caring for people with Alzheimer's Disease and related dementias. She also realised that it was not just those suffering from this terrible disease that needed support; it was also the carers. She knew that many in the community didn't understand this dreaded form of dementia, and so she set about getting the message out to the community by having carers of dementia patients tell their stories to Lions, Rotary, and Probus groups.

It was amazingly successful, and Mum and others established The Speaker's Bureau within the support body Alzheimer's Australia (now called Dementia Australia). But many of the speakers were often elderly people who had never given a speech or presentation in their lives and felt uncomfortable doing so. So what did we do?

At that time, I was teaching presentation skills. There you go. We constructed a presentation workshop for carers. We taught them structure and platform techniques that still gave them the freedom to tell their unique stories in their own unique ways. We didn't simply help create this magnificent army of speakers out there in the community. During those workshops, we listened to each other's stories. Our collective sadness washed over us, and we gained strength in numbers, hope, and conviction we could never have produced had we kept on just doing our own individual things. I'm sure that Speaker's Bureau helped more than just get the word out there. It gave those carers a purpose beyond just being carers.

In 2000, for recognition of her contributions to Alzheimer's Australia amongst other community groups, Mum was asked to carry the Olympic Torch up Fullers Bridge in North Ryde, Sydney, Australia. She was such a tiny little thing that the torch was almost as big as her. But her heart was bigger than Phar Lap's (one of Australia's best-known racehorses). My brother and I were so proud. I can remember tears pouring down our cheeks as we celebrated the torch of humanity she held in her tiny hand. Her legacy lived on, and in fact up until her final months, Mum was still on the helpline as a volunteer. It was her way of honouring Dad and giving back at the same time.

Mum used to say, "Get up, get out and get going." Choose a cause you care deeply about and give of your skills, knowledge, and heart.

2. Consider your skills and knowledge

Once you choose your cause, the next step is to list all the skills you can offer. This can be your technical, functional skills and knowledge like IT, HR, legal advice, building, electrical work, or marketing. It can also be soft skills such as training, speaking, and presenting; your network of contacts; advocating; fundraising; coaching; and facilitating.

3. Application and usage

Then do a little ringing around. Go to the charity's website, or set up a time to talk to someone about volunteering your services. As outlined, go with a specific set of skills that you can offer. Our daughter, Ruby, was sick for many years, and although we had never been directly involved with the Starlight Foundation, I saw first-hand in the hospitals the amazing part they played in the kids' emotional well-being and healing. Their mission grabbed me: "Brightening the lives of seriously ill children and their families."

I had a cause that I connected with. I knew I had skills in training, coaching, and facilitation. I rang the people and culture director, Susan Henry, to offer my services. We then agreed on a leadership programme where I could support them. This was the first step we took together. I'm proud to say we are still able to offer our pro bono leadership development services to Starlight in the form of facilitation and coaching. I selfishly know this work has given me more joy, happiness, and meaning than I'll ever be able to contribute back to Starlight.

4. The first step

Once you have all this information, discipline yourself to take the first step. It's usually giving someone a call, organising an initial discussion, or going to their website. It could be participating in a fundraiser such as Starlight Day (Starlight's national fundraising day). But do something. Get going. Build momentum because a little bit of something is better than a lot of nothing.

I can assure you that the satisfaction you'll get from doing good in the world will be one of the best feelings you'll ever experience.

TIME FOR REFLECTION

There are so many ways you can become involved in charity for purpose or community associations (notice I didn't say not-for-profits). As I've outlined, how you do it will depend on your skills, your passions, your background, and how you can contribute. But I've discovered a pattern about myself and community work that just might help you in your search and decisions about how to be involved.

I love using my training background to do pro bono leadership development services for various charities. Although I get a buzz out of this, it's often me doing it on my own.

It can often be the same if you join a charity board. You get together with great people who want to make a great difference. Yet I've found what often happens is certain opportunities present themselves, and then we individually see how we can help.

For example, an evening may be coming up in which you are going to have an auction. We all commit to approaching our contacts and getting auction prizes for the evening. Yet mostly this is us doing things individually and not as a team. We occasionally integrate as a team, and then we disperse back into our day jobs or doing our individual bits for the group cause. That's a workgroup, not a team.

As important as this is, and as connected to your charity's mission as it could be, it can still be a team of great individuals, not a great team. Personally, I've found I give the most and get the most when working over a period of time with others to achieve a particular outcome, be it putting on a charity golf day, organising a gala ball, or selling merchandise with a team on the charity's special day.

Our time as leaders is limited. To me, it makes sense to maximise the impact of this time by collaborating with others on specific events or outcomes. A new school concert hall, a new piece of medical equipment, organising the singing of carols, and putting on a show at a local aged care village. Do something that has an endpoint, something where you can look back and say, "We did that. We made a difference."

Rather than focussing on many possibilities—and believe me, you'll find this with charity work—work together on the one thing and make it brilliant. The big bets.

Then move on to the next thing, and so on. You'll be amazed at not only the impact you will have but also the personal satisfaction and meaning you'll get when you clearly see a line of sight between your efforts and your outcome.

> *"Never doubt that a small group of thoughtful, committed citizens can change the world; indeed, it's the only thing that ever has."*
> Margaret Mead

SEVENTH WEEK: SMALL TWEAK 7

Follow the four steps outlined and do them now! No excuses, no ifs, no buts. You can make a difference to our world. We need you and your skills. The time really is now. Your successes in business will never ever eclipse the joy, the sense of contribution, the meaning you will get from leading in your community. More than ever, this will be your greatest legacy, the true legacy of *Leaders for Life*.

HONOUR YOUR CALLING

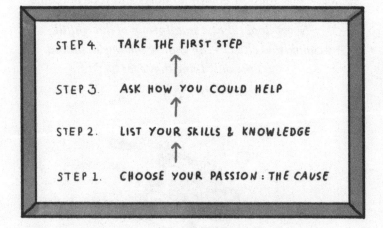

PART 3
KEEP
POLISHING

SO WHAT WILL YOUR LEGACY BE?

Now that you've polished all seven facets of *Your Leadership Diamond*, what's next? What will your legacy be?

This question is often asked of senior leaders when they're presenting on our longer-term leadership development programmes. Most struggle with it unless they've given it some serious thought, and even then, it's often a difficult one to grasp.

Artists have it easy; leaders not so much. The great thing about being an artist, even a starving one, is you do leave behind a legacy of some sort—a piece of art, some poetry, some music, something tangible by which we can remember you. Not so with corporate leaders, or rarely. Not all of us will get to build a Disneyland or create an iPhone. Our legacies will often be much more intangible.

WHAT DO YOU WANT TO BE REMEMBERED FOR?

I also struggle with this question. I get the essence of it, yet it always feels to be loaded with a dose of hubris. On the other hand, there's nothing worse than a leader who sets out to be seen as a great leader rather than creating or accomplishing something of greatness. There's a big difference here.

Yet there is still some magic in the question because it gets you to stop, reflect and gain clarity on what you really stand for and what's really important to you.

> *"If you've got nothing worth dying for,*
> *you've got nothing worth living for."*
> Martin Luther King Jr.

In this way, I believe it makes you stronger, more certain, more committed, and more energised.

Where will your legacy live? It may not be the new product, a new division, new channels, new customers, new service, or the new organisational transformation you pioneered. It will be with the fabulous people you've trained, nurtured, and coached to reach their full potential.

In fact, I'm sure there comes a time in every leader's life where they get more of a buzz out of someone else's achievements than they do from their own. It's the ultimate in going from success to significance, in taking people to a better place.

My advice to you is don't get too hung up on your legacy, but do focus on the number of people's lives you can impact as a leader, the difference you can make to their careers and their lives, through polishing all facets of *Your Leadership Diamond.* In that way, your legacy lives on in their hearts until the last person you touched leaves this world.

My grandfather, Pa, was a very ordinary bloke. Yet his legacy as a leader in my life lives on. I still find myself quoting the many sayings he taught me, and I find myself living my life based on his wisdom.

"Make every post a winning post." (Pa was a bookmaker's clerk)

"Save for a rainy day, but don't miss all the sunshine." (Compound interest in a nutshell)

"Go out on a limb; that's where all the fruit is." (The risk/ reward ratio)

I could go on for many pages. But now, as I pass these sayings and their inherent philosophies onto my son, friends, and coaching clients, Pa's legacy lives on.

WHAT'S YOUR LEADERSHIP LEGACY GOING TO BE?

If you're going to think, think big. Think about some huge social problem you would love to see vanish. What could this be for you? What is something in the world, even beyond your community work, that is so huge it's scary to even think about starting to solve it? It's so big that all the day-to-day challenges, hassles, and problems you experience would feel absolutely insignificant compared to the grandeur of your endeavour.

> *"Don't let complexity stop you. Be activists.*
> *Take on the big inequities. It will be one of the*
> *great experiences of your lives."*
> Bill Gates

Are you thinking big enough? Do you approach every day by wondering how your software could totally transform not just businesses but people's lives?

Do you ever wonder how the products you are creating or marketing could cure world hunger, or could cure the hygiene problems in the world?

One way of arriving at this purpose and rising above the daily tactical challenges is to ask "the foundation question."

And what's that? Well, if like Bill Gates you had all the money in the world (over $100 billion at last count, having given away almost $US50 billion at the time of this writing), and you were to set up a foundation that would focus on curing a major issue in the world—something that could totally alter the way we live, connect, and perform—what would it be? Where would you invest your money, your reputation, your heart and soul?

It's a provocative question, isn't it? You don't have to answer it right now, but please think about it. Sit with it. With this mission in mind, not only will you think about a bigger game, but it could transform the way you approach both your role as a leader and your life.

It's why after all our Leadership Development Programmes, I encourage participants to deeply reflect on what they have learnt, and what they are going to do. If they're thinking "*I'll go back to my workplace and be a better leader*", I respectfully provoke them to go to a higher level. Their goal needs to transcend being (or being seen to be) a great leader. Because, the whole point of being a great leader is to achieve something of greatness. Big difference. Your title makes you a manager, but it's your purpose that makes you a leader. So always make your purpose greater than your paycheck. And whatever you decide your legacy is going to be, I can promise you this. If you get to the end of your days and you can look back knowing you've made a difference, then you'll know you've truly lived.

> *"The greatest thing you'll ever learn, is just to love and be loved in return."*
> From the song Nature Boy recorded by Nat King Cole

FINAL FOOD FOR THOUGHT

You've finished the book. Congratulations. At the end of your seven-week programme, God only knows what madness is occurring in our world. It's so easy to become cynical and to think you can't make a difference. Don't fall into that trap.

Your efforts count, however small they may appear. Cynicism is sometimes an unconscious way of justifying not doing anything. You'll rarely hear it from people who are making a difference in the world, who are getting in there and doing stuff.

There is much to be done—fixing our environment, saving our forests, saving certain species, looking after our at-risk children, supporting the homeless and the landless, the elderly, overcoming terrorism, curing diseases, driving out inequalities of all sorts. But we are making progress.

Be a leader of optimism and abundance, not pessimism and scarcity. That's what our world needs.

Andrew Harvey, in his ground-breaking book *The Hope*, leads us sometimes forcefully (and sometimes gently by the hand) to get in touch with our own suffering. As leaders, we will suffer: the negative politics, the betrayals at work, being passed over for a certain promotion, a dismissal, not receiving the promised bonus, not being given the resources or support you asked for. And then there's our personal lives: the illnesses, the ageing of parents, the break-ups, the divorces, the death of loved ones.

Andrew asks us to look for the lessons here, to look for the meaning. In doing so, we can develop a deeper sense of our own humanity and compassion. That in turn often inspires us to see what good we can do in our world on a global stage. How can we make certain causes sacred and then take some action towards their resolution? He calls this sacred activism.

Perhaps your sacred activism as a leader will be your greatest calling, your greatest sense of contribution and meaning.

"I don't know what your destiny will be, but one thing I know: the only ones among you who will be really happy are those who have sought and found how to serve."
Albert Schweitzer

Peter Diamandis and Steven Kotler, throughout their books *Abundance* and *Bold*, similarly encourage us to set a massively transformative purpose, a singular authentic vision that will give you the emotional energy to push through any barriers. This is so that you get up in the morning full to the brim with possibilities and potential. Be ready to follow with a huge, tangible goal—what they call your moonshot.

My wish for you is that this book and these ideas have in some way served you and helped you find your sacred place, your massively transformational purpose, your moonshot. I sincerely hope you incorporate the techniques outlined into your leadership. That you and your accountability buddy grow over the seven weeks of implementing your tweaks, and that you are better leaders and better people for the experience.

I'd love to hear about how you have supported each other and applied these ideas to your leadership at work, at home, and in your communities. Send an email to *the human enterprise.* You'll find our details at the end of the book.

May you forever polish *Your Leadership Diamond* and let your leadership light shine.

Until we connect again...

Find the passion.
Develop the skills.
Make the numbers.
Make a difference.

Paul "Mitch" Mitchell

YOUR LEADERSHIP DIAMOND: WEEKLY SELF ASSESSMENT

	Week 1	Week 2	Week 3	Week 4	Week 5	Week 6	Week 7
TWEAK 1: Being present							
TWEAK 2: Giving 1 Credit a Day							
TWEAK 3: Setting and Sticking to Ground Rules							
TWEAK 4: Actions for Client Care							
TWEAK 5: 5 Questions for Whole Systems Thinking							
TWEAK 6: "Call a Friend" & Diarise Family Time							
TWEAK 7: 4 Steps to Honour your Calling							

Degree of Focus

Not at all		Some		Moderate		A great deal		Real Strong	
1	2	3	4	5	6	7	8	9	10

Using the scale, score yourself in the table above. One number per week for each tweak.

ACKNOWLEDGEMENTS

There are so many people to acknowledge here. Just as it takes a whole village to raise a child, it takes a whole universe to write a book.

So, a few blanket acknowledgements. First of all, to all the clients whom I've learnt so much from along the way.

To all those whom I've studied with and learnt from over the years: the authors, the trainers and my own personal coaches. Thank you. And to the clients who gave me feedback on the initial manuscript; that means so much to me.

Special thanks to Lynn Johnson and Belinda Ward for your patience in helping with the initial draft of the book. Your understanding of my hieroglyphics is a rare gift.

To Dani Hair for bringing her magic artistry to the illustrations throughout.

To my son, Abe. Without your entrepreneurial zeal and persistence, this book would still be an unfinished manuscript.

And to all the members of *the human enterprise* community, our clients, our consultants, and our suppliers. Truly no one makes it on one's own.

ACKNOWLEDGEMENTS FOR THE SECOND EDITION

There have been so many people I've learnt from over the years that I'd like to acknowledge in this second edition. Sue Hilton, wherever you are, who mentored me as a School Counsellor. John Dyer who took a chance on me at GIG, and Jo-anne Quirk, whose trust in me I'll never forget. At St George, Jim and Margaret Sweeney, what a dynamic duo you were. Your belief in leadership development has made St George what it is today. At Price Waterhouse, my Partner Bruce Clarke who taught me the importance of billing. My old mate Bob Neil, whose sage wisdom I've never forgotten; "a true potential champion".

And then to the many mentors along the way. Robert Kiyosaki, Marvin Oka, Pip Bond, Colin James, Cindy Tonkin, Alan Parker, Matt Church, Marvin Weisbord, Barry and Karen Oshry, Dr Fred Grosse and Dr Ichak Adizes. To our new publisher for the second edition at Woodslane Publishing. Dave and Andrew, it means the world to us that you understand the importance of leading in all aspects of our lives. Finally, like dessert, I've left the best till last. To my soul partner Deborah of over 40 years, for your constant love and support, down to correcting all the typos.

REFERENCES

Adizes, Ichak. *Mastering Change: The Power of Mutual Trust and Respect in Personal Life, Family Life, Business and Society.* The Adizes Institute, 1992.

Biddulph, Steve. *Raising Boys.* Fourth edition. Finch Publishing, 2013.

Blanchard, Ken & Johnson, Spencer. *The One Minute Manager.* William Morrow & Co, 1982.

Block, Peter. *The Empowered Manager: Positive Political Skills at Work.* Second Edition. Wiley, 2016.

Buckingham, Marcus & Coffman, Curt. *First, Break All the Rules.* Simon & Schuster, 1999.

Canfield, Jack & Switzer, Janet. *The Success Principles: How to Get from Where You Are to Where You Want to Be.* Tenth anniversary edition. William Morrow & Company, 2015.

Collins, James & Porras, Jerry. *Built to Last: Successful Habits of Visionary Companies.* HarperCollins Publishers.

Covey, Stephen. *The 7 Habits of Highly Effective People: Powerful Lessons in Personal Change*. Free Press, 1989.

Diamandis, Peter & Kotle, Steven. *Abundance: The Future Is Better Than You Think*. Free Press, 2012.

Diamandis, Peter & Kotle, Steven. *Bold: How to Go Big, Create Wealth and Impact the World*. Simon & Schuster, 2016.

Gallwey, Timothy. *The Inner Game of Golf*. United States: Random House, 2009.

Gerber, Michael. *The E-Myth: Why Most Small Businesses Don't Work and What to Do about It*. Harper Business, 1986.

Godin, Seth. *Purple Cow: Transform Your Business by Being Remarkable*. New Edition. Portfolio, 2009.

Goffee, Robert & Jones, Gareth. *Why Should Anyone Be Led by You: What It Takes to Be an Authentic Leader*. Harvard Business Press, 2006.

Goldsmith, Marshall & Reiter, Mark. *Triggers: Creating Behaviour That Lasts—Becoming the Person You Want to Be*. Crown Business, 2015.

Greenleaf, Robert. *Servant Leadership: A Journey into the Nature of Legitimate Power and Greatness*. Paulist Press, 1977.

Grosse, Fred. *Black Belt of the Mind: A Conscious Approach to a Magnificent Life*. Conscious Wealth Press, 2005.

Harvey, Andrew. *The Hope: A Guide to Sacred Activism*. Hay House, 2009.

Herzberg, Frederick & Mausner, Bernard & Snyderman, Barbara. *The Motivation to Work*. Taylor & Francis, 1959.

Katie, Byron. *Loving What Is: Four Questions That Can Change Your Life*. Harmony Books, 2002.

Kipling, Rudyard. *"If—" Rewards and Fairies*. Doubleday, Page & Company, 1910.

Lee, Harper. *To Kill a Mockingbird*. J. B. Lippincott & Co, 1960.

Mace, Nancy & Rabins, Peter. *The 36-Hour Day*. Warner Books, 1984.

Maister, David. *Managing the Professional Services Firm*. Simon & Schuster, 1997.

Maister, David & McKenna, Patrick. *First Among Equals: How to Manage a Group of Professionals*. The Free Press, 2002.

O'Hern, Nick. *Tour Mentality: Inside the Mind of a Tour Pro*. Self-Published, 2016.

Oshry, Barry. *Seeing Systems: Unlocking the Mysteries of Organizational Life*. Second edition. Berrett-Koehler Publishers, 2007.

Peck, M. Scott. *The Road Less Travelled: A New Psychology of Love, Traditional Values and Spiritual Growth*. Simon & Schuster, 1978.

Raimundo, Carlos. *Relationship Capital: True Success through Coaching and Managing Relationships in Business and Life*. Pearson Education Australia, 2002.

Rice, Christopher & Marlow, Fraser & Masarech, Mary Ann. *The Engagement Equation: Leadership Strategies for an Inspired Workforce*. John Wiley & Sons, 2012.

Ruiz, Don Miguel. *The Four Agreements: A Practical Guide to Personal Freedom*. Amber-Allen Publishing, 1997.

Sinek, Simon. *Start with Why: How Great Leaders Inspire Everyone to Take Action*. Portfolio, 2009.

Ware, Bronnie. *The Top 5 Regrets of the Dying: A Life Transformed by the Dearly Departing*. Hay House, 2012.

Weisbord, Marvin. *Productive Workplaces: Organizing and Managing for Dignity, Meaning, and Community*. Jossey-Bass, 1991.

Wheatley, Meg. *Leadership and the New Science: Discovering Order in a Chaotic World*. Third edition. Berrett-Koehler Publishers, 2006.

Willink, Jocko and Babin, Leif. *Extreme Ownership: How US Navy SEALs Lead and Win*. St. Martin's Press, 2015.

ABOUT THE AUTHOR

Paul Mitchell has been inspiring leaders in all walks of life for over thirty-five years. His unique background in education, psychology, and business has seen him become an authority and trusted colleague to some of Asia-Pacific's most senior leaders.

As the managing director and founder of *the human enterprise*, he has always had one simple and clear message: you can create great enterprises and still make them truly human.

He has two main areas of focus. One is inspiring leaders at every level of the organisation, irrespective of their position or title, to take full responsibility for their own lives and for total organisational results. The other is encouraging leaders to lead in all areas of their lives, not just business. These core beliefs have seen him deliver leadership coaching services, development programmes, facilitation, and keynotes in over fifteen countries with well over ten thousand leaders.

Paul has a bachelor's in social science, a master of arts in psychology, and a diploma of education. He is a founding member of The Interest Group in Coaching Psychology in Australia, as well as a certified Marshall Goldsmith Executive Coach.

Paul lives in Sydney with his wife, Deborah, and is passionate about family, golf, snow skiing, surfing, great music, the arts, and the leadership mindset. His charity of choice is Starlight Children's Foundation Australia, where he served as a NSW advisory board member for over six years; he continues to provide pro bono leadership development services.

HOW CAN WE HELP?

the human enterprise works with individuals, teams, departments, divisions, and organisations to help them build their leadership capacity and capability. But it's more than just leadership skills. We partner with our clients to embed leadership at every level into their cultures. It's about having everyone, regardless of their title or position, develop a leadership (ownership) mindset and taking responsibility for overall total organisational results. That way we all feel inspired to create the most meaningful and productive workplaces on the planet. It's what we call the human enterprise.

TRANSFORMATIONAL LEADERSHIP COACHING
WITH PAUL MITCHELL

Are you a senior executive or director looking to take yourself and your organisation to new heights? This coaching is specifically designed for senior leaders who want to challenge themselves, get to the core of who they are as leaders, and develop the behaviours that will take their organisation to new levels of success. It's about making great leaders even better.

Paul Mitchell is one of Asia-Pacific's foremost leadership coaches. He has coached and mentored hundreds of senior leaders across the region and helped them energise themselves, their teams, and their organisations. He incorporates the trusted technology of Marshall Goldsmith with the unique combinations of *the human enterprise's* inner and outer game approach.

Marshall Goldsmith Stakeholder Centred Coaching has been proven to enable successful people to lead more passionately through long-term change in leadership behaviour by using a methodology that is highly effective and time efficient. The Stakeholder Centred Coaching process guarantees measurable leadership growth and behavioural change.

Transformational Leadership Coaching with Paul Mitchell is not for the faint-hearted. Together, you will take a deep dive on who you are, where your behaviour comes from, and who you need to be in all areas of your life, business, family, and community.

LEADERSHIP DEVELOPMENT PROGRAMMES

You can manage systems and processes as much as you like, but people need to be led. Leadership development programmes with *the human enterprise* provide you with a proven framework for developing your leadership talent and shaping a culture that cultivates leadership skills at every level.

BASECAMP: LEADERSHIP ESSENTIALS
Real Skills for Future Leaders

Inspire new levels of leadership in your Organisation in just one day. We've researched the absolute essentials of inspiring leadership and created a one-day experience for emerging and new leaders or those that need to reconnect to the real difference they can make in your organisation. It's primarily skills based, yet also inspires your associates to be the best leaders they can be at work, at home and in their community. This is achieved through a mixture of content, skills practise, group discussion and personal reflection on some of the key skills required to develop productive passionate workplaces. *Basecamp: Leadership Essentials* enables you to make your continued ascent. It provides you with a solid platform of self-awareness, a servant leadership mindset, and the skills necessary to get to Higher Ground in the future.

HIGHER GROUND
Transforming Good Managers into Great Leaders

Higher Ground is not a one-off training programme. It's a process. It combines the best of our leadership development, coaching, and facilitation services to provide your leaders with the most inspiring customised leadership training in the Asia-Pacific. It's perfect for organisations who want to make leadership part of their culture. If you want to change organisational performance, you have to change people's behaviours.

THE ORGANISATION WORKSHOP
Creating Partnership across Boundaries

The Organisation Workshop is a one- to two-day programme specifically designed to break down organisational silos. Based on the work of Dr Barry Oshry from *Power and Systems*, it brings together all parts of your organisation (your whole system) and sheds a light on the unique challenges faced at each level (top, middle, bottom, and customer). It helps people remove the blinkers and instantly see how organisations really work, instilling in participants a sense of personal responsibility for building better relationships up, down, and across your organisation.

OUR BEST
Transforming High Performing Individuals into a High-Performance Team

Designed for intact teams, Our Best takes the guesswork and assumptions out of team relationships. It provides a foolproof system for understanding each other and breaking down any barriers to effective collaboration. Moving beyond the typical team-bonding exercises, it gets your team to establish an inspiring vision for the future, a mission to be proud of, and ground rules for relating to each other in the context of achieving incredible results.

COME TOGETHER
When Cultures Meet

If a recent merger or acquisition has disrupted the status quo in your organisation, this one-day programme can help. Based on the work of Dr Barry Oshry from *Power and Systems*, Come Together is a unique leadership development experience that gives recently merged organisations or teams a system for bridging any interpersonal gaps between each culture, allowing you to fully maximise the synergies of the merger. It builds a robust culture that is much stronger than the sum of its parts.

WHY SHOULD ANYONE BE LED BY YOU?
What It Takes to Become an Authentic Leader

When business results depend on leading others, it helps to understand what followers need. Yet too many leaders emulate celebrity CEOs or bosses they admire, trying to be people they aren't. As a result, they often fail. If your leaders fail, your organisation will too. Based on the work of London Business School Professors Goffee and Jones, this BlessingWhite programme allows leaders to remain true to who they are while simultaneously modifying their behaviours to respond to the needs of their followers and the circumstances they encounter. They are then able to be more themselves with skill, releasing and focusing amazing amounts of energy to create amazing results.

LEADERSHIP FACILITATION

Bringing your team or organisation together for a strategic initiative off-site? Sure, it's great to get out of the office for a day or so, but for your substantial time and dollar investment, you want to see some tangible results and real behavioural change.

Our facilitation services are designed to help your group, large or small, keep focussed, drive for results, and connect in a way that really gets to the core of why you're coming together in the first place.

Grow a high-performance team built on mutual trust and respect, and see your results soar.

KEYNOTES AND KEYSHOPS™

Want to add even more value to your next conference, off-site, or customer-nurturing event? A keynote from Paul Mitchell will not only lift your audience's energy but will also inspire them to even greater levels of personal and professional success. Our two-hour sessions combine information and application in what we call keyshops.

Paul's leadership keynotes include:

- The Energy Edge
- Taking a Leadership Stand
- Your Leadership Shadow
- Why Should Anyone Be Led by You?
- Feedback: The Breakfast of Champions

YOUR CONTINUED DEVELOPMENT

Your Leadership Diamond is one of many leadership products being developed by *the human enterprise*. Keep a lookout for upcoming products by subscribing to our *Leaders for Life Community*. You can do this via our website. It's absolutely free. You'll learn practical strategies to give you more energy, greater optimism, more resilience, and brilliant results as you lead authentically in your personal and professional life, making a difference way beyond the bottom line. Subscribe now to receive our latest articles and videos, and to listen to our podcast, *Leaders for Life Radio*.

For more information, visit our website:
www.thehumanenterprise.com.au

If you have any questions about the next steps
in your leadership development,
e-mail soul@thehumanenterprise.com.au
or call us at +61 2 9905 5535.

DOWNLOAD THE AUDIOBOOK FOR FREE!

To say thank you for buying my book, I would like to give you the Audiobook version for FREE!

TO DOWNLOAD GO TO:

https://yourleadershipdiamond.com/audiobook

ALSO AVAILABLE FROM WOODSLANE PRESS

Rough Diamonds
by Paul Mitchell

Rough Diamonds is a selection of articles from leadership coach, author and founder of the human enterprise, Paul Mitchell. Building on the advice in his first book, *Your Leadership Diamond*, and following the same 7-facet structure, this compilation is for busy leaders who often don't have major chunks of time free for reading, and who aren't too linear in nature. Even reading one chapter a day gives a great boost. Some chapters are short and sweet, some are much longer. Some outline specific actions or small tweaks, and some just leave you to reflect.

ISBN: 9781925868432

$24.99

If your local bookshop or on-line store does not have stock of this, or any Woodslane Press book, they can easily order it for you. In case of difficulty please contact our customer service team on 02 8445 2300 or info@woodslane.com.au .

NOTES

NOTES

NOTES